CW01661903

100 HYPERLINKS TO THE WORLD OF WORK FOR STUDENTS, JOB SEEKERS AND ENTREPRENEURS.

By Michael Edge

I hear and I forget, I see, and I remember, I do, and I understand. — CONFUCIUS

Disclaimer

The author assumes no responsibility or liability for any errors or omissions whatsoever in the content of this book nor those contained on any website referred to herein. All websites are referred to in good faith and the author does not assume any liability or responsibility for the safety of any website or hyperlink referred to or contained herein. The user shall be totally and solely responsible for interacting with any hyperlink or website content. All information is provided on an "as is" basis with no guarantees of completeness, accuracy, usefulness or timeliness"

INTRODUCTION

NOVEMBER

Wednesday 15th November

While diarising the first two years of my business start-up, I realised that I might be able to paint a picture for students, jobseekers and entrepreneurs to illustrate how every business, large medium or small, is interacting with others to create products or services that people need and are willing to pay for. When we work, we all fit somewhere into a vast economic landscape. According to the Office for National Statistics (1) the estimated number of vacancies in the UK from June to August 2024 was 857,000. In short, businesses in every sector are crying out for people like you who are willing to work. So, I'm now able to provide you with more than 100 Hyperlinks that I've carefully researched on your behalf, which I hope you will find both useful and informative.

For example, the following link will help you understand the business sector and how economies operate (2). Click on the website headings for an abundance of information if you are interested in this topic. For industry specific information why not try Wikipedia for example News media (3). Just open Wikipedia (4) and enter the business sector followed by 'industry' for example Electronics, Energy, Healthcare, Food, Music, Hospitality, Transport, Telecommunications, Aerospace and Agriculture In the UK, the education industry (6) generates more than £20 billion for the economy each year. How on earth does it do that you may be asking?

Perhaps you are a parent, or a teenager about to leave school; if so, you may like to visit 'The Education Hub'. School leaving age – what are your options? (7) You can search on Gov.UK for more than 5,000 apprenticeships (8) available across the UK (just click on Job Categories). Job Centre Plus (9) and many other organizations are more than happy to provide help for those wishing to start their own business. The register of UK regulated professionals and their Regulators (10) will also provide more ideas to help you.

Maybe you left full-time education some years ago and now want to make a fresh start by moving into a new industry sector. Like many, when I reached my 40s, I decided that I needed to learn some new skills, so returned to academic study. Following this I began to teach in the post-compulsory education sector. I then studied Politics and Economics with the Open University to gain a Diploma in Higher Education. Eventually I was drawn to inventing which ticked all the right boxes.

So, if you're curious to know what it might be like to start your own business, or if you simply have a desire to learn more about the world of work, you've come to the right place.

By browsing through my start-up diary, you'll come to appreciate how millions of workers and their jobs are interconnected. More particularly, I've included numerous links to help you choose a career path if you haven't already found one. By clicking on more than one hundred hyperlinks, you should have a greater understanding of what your friends and neighbours are doing when they go to work.

Records show that on average there are approximately 5.7 million private sector businesses in the UK, of which 60% are sole proprietors, 7% partnerships and 33% actively trading Limited Companies. Because of the high failure rate - half UK start-ups fail within 5 years, 3 if you're in London - it's obviously prudent for anyone considering a new business venture to avoid wasting money (during phase one my budget is just over £1,000) and involve themselves in a lot of research, to assess the viability of their proposed project. Many people would call this 'market research plus'.

For anyone aiming to create a high growth start-up or grow an established business, I've covered some topics, such as Companies House rules (for UK Limited Companies) and for His Majesty's Revenue and Customs (HMRC) in some detail, because adhering to the rules is easier than you might expect with the right information.

Some links may have been updated over time, so I suggest that you type any key words into their 'search' facility.

A few links to YouTube videos (to which I have no affiliation) have been included, but as these cannot be reached from a standard Kindle reader, I have pointed you in the right direction.

Kindle Fire etc. and smartphones seem to connect well although you may need to download the YouTube App. Please don't forget to download the Kindle App to your laptop as well.

Here are a few examples of interesting websites that have been helpful to me, and you will come across them in the diary at the appropriate time. The Northern Ireland Business Information Service (11) hosts a lot of helpful videos and other information. How long do large retailers normally take to pay their invoices? (12) is something that may be of interest too. The following website belonging to Lancashire company Booths Supermarket (13) explains step by step how to sell to them, set your recommended retail price (RRP) and wholesale price etc.

Career guidance is not always consistent, so I've embedded some hyperlinks on topics that I've researched on your behalf as I go along. Some of these link to FREE online courses, for example, English, Maths and Computing; job descriptions and opportunities (with salaries). The Kings Trust (113) (121) (149) and how to become an actor (53) just for starters. By the end of this book, I expect you will have a good idea about what interests you and how to achieve your ideal job. Perhaps you will become an entrepreneur and transform yourself into a small business owner like me. As you can imagine, working for yourself can be extremely enjoyable in many ways, because it gives you the freedom to make your own decisions.

For potential entrepreneurs in receipt of Universal Credit, or perhaps I mean Jobseeker's Allowance, any claimant with a genuine desire to start up their own business can convey this to their Job Centre Plus coach who will provide support.

You can read all about moving from Benefits to Work here on the GOV.UK website (14) and it's worthwhile spending some time clicking on the links especially if you're looking for an apprenticeship (15) and want to know what's involved. It appears that the Ministry of Defence provides civilian apprenticeships (16) in a broad range of specialities which may be of interest.

It really isn't difficult to do your own research on the jobs market.

For example if you would like to work with horses or just want to learn more, visit the Horses Fact Book.

Or you could simply type I want to work with People into your browser to learn about 15 options you may wish to consider.

Perhaps you want to work in the food industry if so click here for some ideas.

You could search JobsMedical.co.uk if working in the health sector might interest you.

Just type in - I want to work in the countryside, in the hospitality sector; with animals, in the travel industry, with cars, with aircraft, with boats, with children, with plants, with money; you name it and all the information is here online.

A quick tip is to find out all you possibly can about the company you may want to join and their business sector, prior to attending an interview. What you learn will also help you to prepare an impressive CV and show a potential employer that you understand their industry. For example: if you want to drive trains you could start here. Don't be put off if some training is required because you are bound to reach your goal in the end.

Billions of people worldwide are working to earn enough to achieve a good standard of living for themselves and their families. This also means that most of us, in western economies, are paying some form of income tax to cover the cost of public services such as the National Health Service – (see here for nursing vacancies (17)) and education for ourselves and our children; services that we probably couldn't afford to pay for as individuals. Most people in work started their careers by learning a skill that they 'hopefully' enjoyed and are now selling to those who need their knowledge and will pay for it! Sometimes it's hard to know where we fit into all this.

To make it easy to skim read, I've typed the first sentence of each paragraph in italics. If you're reading on Kindle which is where you will gain the most benefit, you may want to use the Notebook and other great features. The Kindle 'search' function is also very useful and of course, all hyperlinks are clickable. A few of the search words you may wish to use in this book which will take you to the subject that is of interest (internal book links) might be 'apprenticeships', 'business sector', 'careers', 'finance', 'FREE', 'innovation', 'job descriptions', 'job vacancies', 'lectures', 'Open University', 'patents', 'rules', 'selling', and 'support'.

Working for yourself on a self-employed basis, is one option, but if your intention is to grow a business, it's worth knowing what might be involved. Therefore, many of the topics in my diary relate to sole proprietors and partnerships as well as Limited Companies.

If you eventually decide that you want to set up in business as a sole-trader you could start by looking on the Companies House website (18). If you want to set up a Partnership (19) look here. To set up a Limited Company (20) you'll need to click here.

Throughout this book I've referred to the product as my 'gadget' so that the reader won't be distracted.

This is a diary about my journey, my effort, my World of Work and my story begins here.

The Limited Company (my start-up business), which is the subject of this diary, will be trading as a general commercial wholesaler, as it's a model that I understand from experience.

My financial strategy will be to ask my main suppliers, in this case those supplying the removable parts and the assembly and packaging services, to grant a minimum of 30 days credit, which is not always available to a company without a documented trading history.

I shall also be asking my bank for a 'factoring' or 'invoice discounting' facility to help with cash flow. This will mean that as soon as an order is delivered to my customer and invoiced by me, I can draw down (borrow) a percentage of the total invoice value (including the VAT) which is usually between 70% - 80%. I shall then be able to pay my suppliers quickly, thereby never exceeding their payment terms. This is because some companies are known for taking two months or longer to settle their accounts. You can find out how long some of the larger companies usually take by looking on the GOV.UK (21) website. I'm drawn to invoice discounting because it's a 'no sale – no loan' arrangement. From my point of view, it's a sensible cash-flow control mechanism and will stop me from spending money I don't yet have. But at some stage, I shall probably need an investor to get me into the production stage.

Just one of the disincentives to trying to commercialise a newly patented product, (one for which the inventor has, for a limited period, the sole rights to exploit), is that many companies have Innovation Departments devoted to new product development. It should surprise no one therefore, if they eventually get around most patents, so long as the product has enough potential to make money. However, now that everything is being done online, business start-ups can begin quickly which gives inventors a time advantage.

First, I need to continue my online research and generate a fresh business plan which I'll fill with statistics to show how the business will make a profit. I need to identify all my potential customers and suppliers, create forecasts in spreadsheet format for the Cash Flow and Sales Projections, Profit & Loss and Balance Sheet just for starters. I'll find some websites to help you with this topic later.

Friday 18th November

High Street pharmacy targets could be Lloyd's Pharmacy (1,500 outlets), Boots (2,500), Superdrug (900) and Well Pharmacy (770 outlets) previously known as Co-Operative Pharmacy and owned by Bestway. Sangers (less than 100 outlets) and trading under the name Paydens, might also be a good choice. I've just noticed that at the time of writing, Britain's Health and Fitness Club sector is worth an estimated £3.1 billion.

Tuesday 22nd November

Buying a steel or aluminium mould for injection moulding the plastic parts will be very costly at around £12,000, unless the work is commissioned in China. On top of that there will be the cost of the plastic pieces themselves. So, I need to start investigating 3D printing.

I've just carried out a Companies House check on a potential 3D Print Company and have written to them enclosing a rough sketch. I wanted to ask them to sign a Non-Disclosure Agreement (NDA) but finally decided to head my letter 'Confidential' rather than make a fuss. I shall ask them to print the patent number on the item in due course, because if it's highly visible my company will have a serious claim against any infringement should it occur.

Although I've learned to prepare my own patents, my local patent agent has been very helpful over the years. I've chosen a name that is totally unique for my invention because then it can be registered as a Trademark and in due course, I'll be adding the ® symbol to it.

Today I've registered the new company name online at Companies House (22), but before registering I had to download their templates and create a Memorandum of Association (23) and model 'Articles of Association' (24) and make them fit the company. However, first I reminded myself of the responsibilities I would be taking on and took the time to read up on the subject by browsing the Companies House (25) website.

Wednesday 23rd November

I think I would be more than happy to part with 20% of the company for a fair investment and experienced help if it would ensure that I could get going quickly. This time I must concentrate more on the WIFT factor to attract investors, which stands for 'What's in it for them?'

It's been confirmed that my company name has been registered, and I'm asked by Companies House if I want to receive email reminders when the Annual Accounts and Annual Return (now called Confirmation Statement) are due. Naturally I do. Now I'm asked to read a whole load of rules for Directors. So today will be the official starting date for this company's tax accounting period unless I decide to change it.

I'm going to look on YouTube for book-keeping videos for you now as everyone needs to keep on the right side of HMRC and it's always good to keep up to date. HMRC require me to send them a Company Tax Return (26) each year and let them know if the company owes them any corporation tax. This of course means that accounts need to be kept.

I suspect that a lack of skill in this area could be the reason why so many start-ups fail to trade successfully beyond the first 3 - 5 years. For this start-up and those primarily involved in market research and product testing, perhaps with a small amount of trading thrown in, the accounts can usually be generated quite simply by the owner, possibly requiring professional help once established. It's basically about keeping the books up to date. There are plenty of online resources that can be accessed and the Open University (27) provides a FREE online course to help start-up owners or anyone else for that matter, learn about book-keeping.

WARNING: The following can make for somewhat boring reading so unless you want to know more about setting up a company with limited liability, I would advise you to scroll down to the 25th of November.

Whenever a new company is registered at Companies House, His Majesty's Revenue and Customs (HMRC) is automatically informed. HMRC will then send a letter of introduction to the company's Registered Office and provide a 'unique taxpayer reference number'

It's necessary for all private limited companies to register their company on the HMRC (27) website for the following purposes. (1) Submitting the company's Corporation Tax Return (the accounts for taxation purposes); (2) setting up a payment method for Corporation Tax; (3) filing a VAT Return if you have registered for VAT; and (4) notifying HMRC of any other changes they need to be told about. Once registered the company will be sent an 'activation code' by snail mail.

When logging on, a call or text will be received from HMRCs online services, with an access code number. This is for security purposes. See letter from HMRC for your 'unique taxpayer reference number'

HMRC must be informed <u>within three months of registration with Companies House,</u> if the company is not trading (dormant).

If the company is trading, then HMRC must be advised <u>within three months of starting to trade</u> and becoming active. The following link explains the term 'dormant' for <u>Corporation Tax (28)</u> purposes. Once signed in there's a link on the HMRC website where it's possible to let them know that you have (a) stopped, (b) never have, or (c) have started to trade. Alternatively, you can write to your Company Tax Office at the address on their correspondence.

If you've been trading but have stopped doing so, as soon as HMRC receive your notification, they'll send a 'Notice to Deliver a Corporation Tax Return' to your registered office.

HMRC allows <u>one year</u> from the end of your accounting period for you to complete and file your <u>Corporation/Company Tax Return</u>. So, if your accounting period is from 1st January – 31st

December 2018, you will have until 31st December 2019 to file your return (accounts). This should not be confused with the deadline for **paying** your Corporation Tax which is due **three months earlier** with a time limit of **nine months and one day** after the end of the accounting period. Therefore, this would be due for payment no later than 1st October 2019.

Because HMRC's notices for 'Company Tax Return' (the accounts) and 'Request to make your Corporation Tax Payment' are so similar and in rather small print, as soon as they arrive, I highlight the subject so that the two cannot be confused. I then check that the deadline is clearly marked on my calendar and mark up a reminder one month ahead.

I find it's essential to file each communication in date order in a ring binder, otherwise it's virtually impossible to keep track if they become muddled up. I also highlight the date sent (issue date) and the subject of the Notice which is in the top right-hand corner and could be one of the following: 'Corporation Tax – Payment Reminder', Corporation Tax – Notice to Deliver a

Company Tax Return, Corporation Tax – Return and Payment Reminder. There may even be a Corporation Tax header with the subject being within the body of the letter such as 'formal notice of a penalty determination'.

It's worth noting that HMRC will apply financial penalties (29) should company owners fail to notify them about something they need to know, with further information here (30). For more detail see the HMRC Compliance Handbook (31).

Companies House will want something a little different called the Annual Accounts (32). This link takes you to a page headed 'Prepare Annual Accounts for a Private Limited Company' they are also referred to as 'Statutory Accounts'. Once again, submitting this information is a legal requirement

It's probably easiest to submit the Annual Accounts (for Companies House) and Corporation Tax Return (for HMRC) simultaneously online. 'Accounts and Tax Return for Private Limited Companies (33)' and 'File Your Accounts and Tax Return'(34). The data you'll need to enter online must be taken from your Annual/Statutory Accounts, which you'll need to prepare first using your financial records. You'll need to give a copy of these to all your shareholders, if you have any. This is the data that you'll need to complete your Corporation Tax Return for HMRC. If you want to complete your accounts for Companies House (33) first (which are due 3 months before the Tax Return) this is very quick and easy to do – the other being quite long. Because there are so many links, ID and other numbers involved with these Government websites I thoroughly recommend making meticulous notes so that you don't waste time re-learning what to do next. Don't be too worried about the accounts though, because the first year you are very likely to be what is called a micro-entity (35).

Furthermore, even if the company is dormant, it's still necessary to submit the Annual Accounts and a Confirmation Statement (Annual Return) to Companies House. See how to file your Confirmation Statement (36) with Companies House.

Companies House can start proceedings to strike the company off the Register, if a company fails to submit all the required documents. They will fine the company £150 if the accounts are filed late, which can increase to £1,500. Read what happened to Sports Direct owner Mike Ashley (37).

Dormant, for Companies House purposes, relates to a company that has had no significant accounting transactions. It's usual to tell Companies House that the company is dormant when filing the Annual Accounts. There's no need to tell them when the company starts trading – see here (38).

It's important to read the following information (39) as it explains the due dates for delivery of the Annual Accounts to Companies house, in addition to what information must be included. Companies have 21 months from the date they register to submit their first accounts to Companies House, thereafter nine months after their financial year end.

Companies House have provided some helpful <u>tips on how to file the Annual Accounts on time (40).</u>

It goes without saying that you'll need to support yourself while all this work is going on. So, I'd like to remind you to be careful when claiming working tax credits because the system is a little complicated. Any over payment will be clawed back by HMRC.

Friday 25th November

The dictionary definition of 'cash book' is 'a book in which receipts and payments of money are recorded'. I've just been watching a video on YouTube by IGCSE which is very helpful. The first video I watched explains very clearly how the most important ledger called the 'cash book' (the books of accounts are known as ledgers), will help the bookkeeper to keep a record of all money coming in and going out

<u>The terms Debit and Credit are used as verbs when used by the bank BUT as nouns when used in the cash book</u>. This can be confusing.

<u>In 'banking' terms</u> the dictionary explains the nature of a **debit** <u>(verb)</u> as **the removal of money from an account** (money going out) and as a **credit** <u>(verb)</u> as **the record of money coming into an account.** A verb is a doing word, an action.

<u>In 'cash book' terms</u> the dictionary explains the nature of a **debit** (noun), (**debits** are entered on the **<u>left</u>** side) as the creation of a record of money that a business has coming in. On the **credit (right)** side of the cash book, this is where the record of all purchases/payments for goods, services, interest on loans, bank charges etc. are made. These entries relate to gains by the company in return for payment (money is going out).

Here are a few recommendations from my Accountant. (1) "Have your bank statements beside you when you make entries into your cash book. Don't use cash or personal credit cards when buying items or services for the company. This makes it much easier to keep the cash book in line with the bank accounts". (2) "Use an analysed cash book. This is where after entering your income or outgoings (in separate columns of course) you then expand the detail – especially for costs – into analysis columns. This will make it much easier to prepare the accounts and when submitting tax returns".

"Generally speaking, I wouldn't recommend the use of an accounting package in the beginning. It's important to get a grip on the numbers and sometimes accounting packages can obscure data by burying it in some part of the system that you're unfamiliar with. You can buy accounting cash books with analysis columns if you want to keep your records manually. Alternatively, you can construct a simple cash book in a spreadsheet such as Excel (Windows) or Numbers (Apple). Free spreadsheets are plentiful. You should keep the books in line with the company bank account on a regular basis; weekly, or even daily if there are a lot of entries being made" End of quote.

Although I only need to balance the books at the end of each month, I can always work out where I am financially, by adding up the credits (on the right) and subtracting them from the debits (on the left) whenever I need to. Although an IGCSE video, shows three column cash being used for discounts, I've found that using the three columns in a slightly different way helps me to work out my VAT return quickly, as well as saving me a lot of time in the first year or two when I shall not expect to give or receive any discounts. I simply use the credit side (right) to put the date, description, folio number which identifies the entry, followed by the purchase price net of VAT, the VAT element (which should be shown separately on all invoices) followed by the total price inclusive of VAT. This way I can quickly add up the VAT each quarter. Naturally, any money, primarily in the form of loans from myself at present, and any VAT rebate going into the company bank account (because I've registered for VAT), is entered on the debit side (left) and the debits and credits for each month are made to balance as shown in the video.

On the radio this morning, I heard mention of some financial help for start-ups so I'm 'searching' 'Chancellor's Statement – help for start-ups'. As usual this money, £400M apparently, is divided up and allocated to various Fund Managers. From what I can see they all require matched funding from another source, often a bank loan or sale of equity. I'm not interested in a bank loan.

I'm still waiting for the 3D Company to get back to me with a quotation. All prices will have delivery and VAT added of course, but I can claim the VAT back on the HMRC website. I prefer to register as early as possible so that I can apply to be reimbursed for the VAT on my start-up costs. Other companies will expect me to be registered anyway.

I've a note saying 'Statement of Compliance' on my desk in relation to the company registration. So, I've 'searched' 'Statement of Compliance for Companies House' and their website came up with a link to loads of useful information. It's the new name for the 'Annual Return (41)'.

It's now OK for me to download a copy of my 'Certificate of Incorporation for a Private Limited Company' which will have the company registration number on it. I see that I must use an Authentication Code to log-on which seems to ring a bell, so I must look out for this as the download service expires in 10 days apparently.

Monday 28th November

I've now checked on the IPO website (42) and it will cost me £170 if I register the trademark online and £200 if I submit a paper application. Since I already own the domains .com and .co.uk I think I'll be safe for a while until I can afford to register the trademark.

I've also searched their site for Draft Licensing Agreements and have found a page full of information.

DECEMBER

Saturday 3rd December

I'm back on the Intellectual Property Office (IPO) website looking for 'infringement of intellectual property. From what I can gather, it's possible to take out 'before the event' insurance, so that if somebody infringes, or I inadvertently infringe another's IP, then my legal expenses and/or those of the other party will be covered. This must be taken out before there is any suspicion of infringement. It's recommended that domestic (UK) cover is taken out first followed by other territories. As I only have a UK patent, this doesn't apply. Excesses which are used to lower the premium usually start at £1,000 it says, which is the amount the company would have to pay in the event of legal action. I would need an insurance broker … etc.

Wednesday 7th December

I sent another letter requesting a quote to the 3D Company on Monday, this time by Special Delivery. I checked with tracking yesterday and found that it had been delivered at 7.30 a.m. and was signed for by Security. I've emailed to ask whether they've received it.

I've been a bit slow over the past few days as I'm waiting for a quote from the 3D Company. The part could be far too expensive for this project to be viable even.

I've saved the NHS Supply Chain (43) link here just in case I need it someday. It appears that the owner of Supply Chain NHS.UK is DHL Supply Chain Limited, in turn owned by the German company Deutsche Post DHL. It says they are the world's largest courier company and the successor to the German Mail Authority following privatization.

Wednesday 14th December

The 3D Company finally got back to me after I'd chased up their Design Department. However, it has been well worth the effort with the delay having been caused by a change of premises. The price for the CAD file is £50 per hour (estimated drafting time 2 hours) and £1 for the prototype. So, this is affordable, although I must consider any extra time spent tweaking the thing.

Tuesday 20th December

I've set out my Business Plan headings so that I can add information as I go along. The list starts with Directors and Advisors and the Executive Summary, which is usually written last of all to summarise the main topics with the audience in mind, often investors or a bank.

Business Angels (sometimes a group) or Venture Capitalists are the usual source of equity finance. Equity finance is that given in return for a share of the company. There are many websites which explain this term. I've checked the UK Business Angel Association (UKBAA) (44) website which is for smallish amounts, and the British Venture Capital Association (BVCA) (45) website just to refresh my memory. Something I've noticed on the Angel website is that there's a regulatory framework for Angel investing and that before a company passes their business plan to a potential Angel investor, they should ensure that the investor has self-certified as either a 'high net worth' or 'sophisticated' investor, as defined by the FCA under the Financial Services and Markets Act 2000 (FSMA).

I've borrowed from the bank previously which was 'interesting' but extremely costly. I've also made presentations to potential Business Angel investors but without much success. I was once told by a fellow seeker of angel capital that he'd just missed a good investment deal because he didn't want to ask his chairman, who was working on a deferred payment basis, to step down so that the investor could replace him. The investor had suggested that the chairman take shares in lieu of deferred remuneration. Because this chap refused, he lost the deal, which sounds as if it would have been a good one because the Angel was a manufacturer and a perfect fit for his company. The product was successful eventually, but not for him.

JANUARY

Sunday 1st January

Yesterday evening I was looking up Intellectual Property (IP) Licensing again to find out whether VAT is payable on the transfer or licensing of IP. I've discovered that it is and that this must be expressed in the agreement under financial details.

I've just checked online and discovered that the Corporation Tax rate is currently 25% if your company made more than £250,000 net profit, or 19% if your company made £50,000 net profit or less. It seems that on profits between £50,000 and £250,000 there is a sliding scale, but you will need to check for yourself.

Tuesday 24th January

I've just received another email from 3D Co. which explains that confidentiality is covered by their Terms and Conditions (T&Cs) already and that they can't publish anything without my permission. So, I've set up an account on their website and await their pro-forma invoice which means I shall have to pay up front; I think it's 50%

in this case, before they are willing to start the design work.

How the process seems to work is that the designer creates a 3D drawing based on the information I've provided. They'll take precise measurements of the sample that I've sent and create a design that should function as requested. Before they print anything, they'll send me a technical drawing for my approval. After the first print, any minor design tweaks needed to improve fit or tolerance would be free, however, reprints would be charged for. I'm happy with this and have responded accordingly

FEBRUARY

Wednesday 1st February

I've suddenly become nervous about the trademark. So, I went to the IPO website and clicked on the trademark link (46). I then searched for my new brand name in all categories. So far it hasn't shown up, but I needed to be sure that no one had registered something similar very recently so went to check the Electronic Trade Marks Journal (47). Once an application has been accepted it's published in here and is easy to find. Everyone is given the opportunity to make comments or objections for up to 2 months. This may be extended to 3 months under certain circumstances. If after the 2 month period nobody has made an objection, then the mark is registered and a certificate dispatched. The protection lasts for 10 years but can be renewed every 10 years until no longer required.

I've been typing up a list of unique selling points (USPs) and have also located a British manufacturing company that appears to make the

second item I'll need to complete the product. This was not easy as so many products are now made in China.

Sunday 5th February

I really must get some sort of website up and running and find out how to produce a video to put on YouTube.

Selling on Amazon for customer convenience is an option. I could either use, what I call their 'shopfront' service, where I would deliver to the customer and invoice them myself, or their fulfilment service, in which case they would do everything, and I'd just need to supply the stock to their warehouse. But perhaps eBay would be the best place to start, as I would only need to carry a small amount of stock, and it seems to be the least expensive option from a start-up perspective.

Friday 10th February

I've now received a CAD file from 3D Co. Incidentally, if you have an interest in a career in computer aided design (CAD) (48), you can find out more on the Prospects website. You can scroll down their A - Z of jobs at Prospects.ac.uk (49) which lists over 100 job profiles from astronomer to zoologist.

If you need some career guidance, you could also visit the BBC A – Z of Careers (50) and maybe jump directly to a career in Civil Engineering (51). Scroll down to watch the video. You could follow this with a visit to Indeed.com (52) to check for current job vacancies and find out what your potential salary might be. For further information about how to become an actor, just for example, you can discover more from a website called the National Careers Service (53). You may also want to look at their Skills Assessment (54) page. Once you've decided what career path you wish to follow, then you could click on the following link if you need to find a course, which is another on the above NCS (55) website. For example, if you want to study Accounting, simply type in your nearest town and 'Accounting' into the box at the top. To find FREE online courses (56) just type in your location and the word FREE into the Course or Keyword box. (I've just found Digital Marketing – I wish I'd spotted this before! It's all online and flexible).You could also try clicking on the same website, then scroll down and click on SKILLS TOOL KIT (57) to find numerous FREE courses such as Maths, Computer Essentials, Business and Finance and many more. I've also found thinkemployment.com. Unfortunately, I couldn't access the courses on my Kindle, but the website worked well on my laptop and probably will on other mobile devices. Just click on Courses at the top. There are four key areas where courses are funded by the Department for Education and are therefore FREE. These are 'Teaching' 'Health and Social' 'Heavy Goods Vehicle Driving' and 'Digital'. I've also found an apprenticeship scheme on a different website for those who want to train in the craft sector worth up to £6,000 p.a. at QUEST (58).

Kick Off in Business (59) sponsored by the government's Department for Business and Trade, provides a FREE, one-week, online business start-up and self-employment course.

Regarding protecting my intellectual property, I've had a look at 3D Co's T&Cs (Terms & Conditions) and found that there's a clause

relating to something called 'Social Postage' which apparently, if I click on a button, (goodness knows whether I have or not as I certainly didn't see it), they have the right to show and distribute images of my design, which is the last thing I want. So, I've held off giving the go ahead until I receive their reassurance and asked – where is this button anyway? As is the usual practice with commissioned photographic or design work, it is the artist/company that undertakes the work, who owns the copyright so far as I understand it and with regard to the CAD design, I can purchase this for a further £200 it seems, or as they say, twice the original cost of the design.

Sunday 12th February

I received the first prototypes yesterday and am very pleased with the appearance although a small adjustment will be needed. I've contacted 3D Co. with the necessary details.

Wednesday 22nd February

I've just ordered some lightweight cartons, but only 30 for the moment so I can experiment with packaging.

Thursday 23rd February

I'm about to look up 'hot foil printing process' on YouTube which may come in handy.

I'm impressed. I ordered white cartons online yesterday and they've just arrived. Since I didn't ask for next day delivery, but they are here nevertheless, they must have put themselves out because I've just registered as a new customer. Good idea.

Today I'm looking for products like mine on 'search images' (better late than never). At first glance there are a few items that could perform a similar function, but my invention is completely different and an original innovation. It's evident from my searches that no one has ever imagined my new product. This is one of the key requirements for being granted a patent in that it must not be obvious.

I've just found my list of countries by English-speaking populations. It lists, among others the USA 96%, UK 97%, Canada 85%, Australia 87%, The Netherlands 87%, Denmark 86%, Norway 91%, Isle of Man 99%, Sweden 89%, Ireland 98%,

New Zealand 97% so these are all export opportunities I should consider.

Monday 27th February

3D Co. is going to make some small adjustments for me. I've been quoted another £40 for the design work, plus £1.00 for the prototype, plus £5.00 postage and packing = £46.00; add VAT £9.20 = £55.20. The invoice was attached to the email, and I was able to click on the 'Xero' link at the top which enabled me to pay immediately with no hassle.

As mentioned, you don't need to register with HMRC for VAT until your company's turnover reaches £90,000. It's quite alarming how much 20% VAT will add to the retail price once a business is registered. Thereafter, VAT must be added to all selling prices, which makes any product a lot more expensive. However, doing the VAT returns online is relatively easy. Accountants, or me in this case, simply fill out a few boxes in relation to UK and non-UK sales and purchases; the lower figure is deducted from the higher and unless I'm claiming a rebate, the balance is then paid to HMRC. (From 1st November, 2022 HMRC required all VAT returns to be made online; they have made tax digital Making Tax Digital – MTD (60)). This requires software, some of which is free and this link will explain more (61) .

I must now try to find another manufacturer as I don't want to leave myself vulnerable to just one supplier.

MARCH

Monday 6th March

Fortunately, I still have the spreadsheets from my last business on a memory stick, which is going to make life a lot easier as I can just copy and edit them. Before I can start work on the financials though, I shall need to work out the cost and selling price of every item. I'll then have to make adjustments for selling on eBay or Amazon, which will require the addition of PayPal fees, an insertion fee for eBay and delivery charges etc.

Wednesday 8th March

I'm in the middle of another Companies House check. Looking at the first filed documents, the company I have approached, must have been a 'ready-made shelf company' which is a quick way to get up and running. In this case an agent will have set up the company with 'any old name' so long as it's not already taken, in anticipation of selling the company on to new business owners who want to get going quickly. In such a case the agent would have fulfilled all the legal requirements and put their own name down as the first Company Secretary. Then the new owners, or the agent, simply register the change of company name and ownership with Companies House and submit the names of the new directors and company secretary, if they choose to have one.

While on the website, I've been reading a few more sets of company accounts as they can be accessed for free. I generally stick to the ones headed Total Exemption Small Company Accounts, although the larger corporate ones can be educational.

I'm retaining my long-suffering Accountant from previous years, although he hasn't had a chance to do much work on the business side of things, except act as the company's registered office and deal with bits and bobs.

Well, these are my notes from the middle of the night. Consider selling 5% equity for a loan of £5,000, repayable at the end of year 3; set up PayPal, Amazon and a company bank account; register for VAT. Check that the full Jiffy bag and carton will go through the slot in my Royal Mail measuring gauge; visit the post office or check online the cost of First Class signed for; investigate vacuum packaging companies and check who makes printed headers with a euro-slot.

I've now finished writing up the Instructions for Use.

Thursday 9th March

I've been exploring Amazon again. When customers click on my product to make a purchase, I'm assuming that they'll be directed to my website, and I'll then need to process and deliver the item; but I need to check how it all works. (It seems that I don't need a website to sell on Amazon).

Assuming that I'm going to sell online, I've checked to see whether the carton is small enough to go through the 'letter rate' slot and discovered that it's too big for large letter and would need to be sent as a 'small package'. So, at a selling price of £16.99 plus delivery of £4.45 = £21.44 then add VAT at 20% £4.29 it would cost the customer £25.73. I think this is too expensive and will require some work. So far as I understand it VAT is charged on the package because it is a 'delivered good' but you had better check here for clarity.

Saturday 11th March

I've managed to find my previous eBay file and think that for small start-up quantities this is probably a better option than Amazon. I now need to open a bank account so that I can set up an account with PayPal, then eBay and register for VAT. I can start very small on eBay buying in a minimal quantity of stock. It seems that it's because I'm a business retailer that the VAT number must be given to eBay, or something. It's not an easy task working out the fees for Amazon and eBay which include VAT. It's the VAT which baffles me and takes up so much time, what has/hasn't got to have it added and at what point in my calculations? I've now looked on YouTube for advice.

Tuesday 14th March

I've just shocked myself and paid £170 to the Patent Office to register my new trademark.

As a potential wholesale operation, one of my fears has always been 'over trading' which

means that I might be unable to finance the production of orders. This could happen if I let customers pay 60 days after delivery but only manage to agree 30 days credit with my suppliers. Also, my customers may not even pay me within the agreed timescale. This is why I've opted for an invoice discounting facility. To refresh my memory I've just done a 'search' and found a very good website which explains how to avoid overtrading (63). Although this is a website for Northern Ireland, it's the best one I've found yet and relates to all UK matters so far as I can tell. The website also has some great videos one of which is 'How to use social media (64). To watch their videos, just type 'video' into the search box. Other useful information relates to creating an innovative start-up (65).

Wednesday 15th March

I think I've gone into the Bank's website via the wrong portal or something. Anyway, I'm interested in the 18 months free banking, hire purchase, overdrafts, invoice finance and credit cards although I probably won't use anything other than the free banking, invoice discounting and just possibly an overdraft facility.

The 3D Co. designer has offered to put my trademark™ onto the product at no extra cost.

Friday 17th March

I've given up trying to register online for a Business Account with my current bank, as their website won't let me get to the end. But as they offer 18 months free banking and the other just 12 months, I'm going to stick with the one I'm familiar with and pay them a visit. From experience I know that 12 months will fly by.

Monday 20th March

I've finally completed my pricing spreadsheet for 'wholesale' having made a few guesses about delivery charges. No one has quoted a minimum order quantity, so I've based my costs on 50 units. Although 3D Co. has offered a quantity discount on 200, I just don't have that kind of money at present. VAT bumps everything up by 20% and I won't recover that for anything up to three months. In total I need about £487 to cover start-up costs.

I'm going to start trading on the 1st May because it will take another month to sort out the bank account and buy in stock.

Wednesday 22nd March

I've just discovered that my application for registration of my brand name has been accepted and will now be published in the online journal for two months. If there are no objections, then the trademark will be granted two weeks after the two-month period ends and a certificate sent to the company. I've signed up for email alerts so that I'll be notified the moment the word gains registered status.

Friday 24th March

I now have a business account. There have been some changes recently in that the Personal Advisors at my bank, are now trained to set up simple business accounts when there's only a single director and anticipated turnover is less than £50,000. As I don't expect to exceed £10K during year one, this suits me perfectly.

When the bank official was asking about any expenses that I'd incurred in setting up the

business, I didn't mention the cost of patenting which was approximately £325 in IPO fees which are exempt of VAT. Because I created the technical data myself, the only cost was in my time and energy but usually starts at about £3,000 if done by a Patent Agent. Nor did I mention the cost of the Trademark registration which was £170 for just one class. This is because the intellectual property belongs to me personally and not the company. If I license the IP later, take out a loan or factor, I shall transfer it to the company, and it will become a company asset. I shall then need to complete the relevant form and submit it to the Patent Office (66).

Thursday 30th March

The bank account is now ready for use which was nice and quick. I received the Visa debit card yesterday. However, having read an article about fraud I shall probably switch to a credit card before very long.

Now I'm going to register for VAT. HMRC runs a scheme (I think it's called Patent Box) whereby profit generated by a company's intellectual property may be charged a corporation tax rate of 10% rather than 20%.

APRIL

Monday 3rd April

Today I've received some interesting information from the IPO. On at least two occasions, I've written to ask why there isn't any data on the number of women inventors in the UK. I've now received a response from the Head of Informatics and Business Intelligence with some useful links. This seems to be the most relevant: "Gender Profiles in UK Patenting: "An Analysis of Female Inventorship" (67).

As I suspected, women are totally underrepresented within this sector with numbers never having exceeded 8.5%. I've scrolled to the bottom of the first document to find legal data and it says that the document is free for re-use under the 'Open Government License' (68).

I haven't seriously considered Licensing intellectual property (69) in the past but if I ever do I'll have a good read.

Tuesday 4th April

Yesterday I dropped in at Superdrug to see where the product might possibly be displayed. I found the right section and now need to create packaging that wouldn't look out of place among these products. I've realized only recently that many items seem to need a euro-slot for hanging on pegs; so, I must work out how to achieve this.

Because I'm using free software now rather than Word, (I purchased MS Office later as it's needed to create a Kindle book), I may need to remind myself how to type the registered symbol ® at some stage. This can be created by holding down Alt and then typing zero one seven four on the number pad. For ™ which is what I'll be using for the time being, I need to hold down Alt and key in zero one five three. Copyright © needs to be put on all printed company material, so I expect to use Alt then zero one six nine regularly.

I've just finished designing my packaging. I'm going to have to contract this element out as piecework. My search for 'piecework UK' (70) has provided me with a link to the GOV.UK website.

It seems that employing people, even for piecework where the work is carried out at home, can be complicated and the company would be responsible for wages, national insurance, pensions and so forth. So, I've shelved the idea until the company starts to prosper.

***Next 'search' is for 'light assembly' and I've found a social enterprise providing employment for adults with mental health issues in the Midlands called** Better Pathways (71)*. I'll keep the link for future reference.

Thinking about factoring, it appears that as soon as the goods are delivered to the customer, they'll need to be invoiced, and a copy sent to my bank's Commercial (factoring) Division. They'll then transfer typically 80% of the invoice value to the company bank account. I can then pay my suppliers quickly and within the 30-day credit limit. I'll need to sort out insurance as well. Factoring (72) is explained on the GOV.UK website.

I need to remember that shelf space is always key to buyer decisions, because they'll need to take something off the shelf before they can put

another product on. However, this may not apply if the goods are only sold online, so long as there's room in their warehouse.

What I'm reading now has just reminded me that I need to have the product checked for quality and safety so I'm looking for some guidance on the GOV.UK (73) website. This is really important information and recommends that wholesalers and retailers take out Product Liability Insurance, just in case of a complaint, although it doesn't appear to be compulsory. For manufacturers though, it seems to be essential. There's also a mention of CE markings and which category of product must display these. Fortunately, my product doesn't appear in any of the categories listed here (74).

I must get some Terms and Conditions drafted soon as I'll need to send these out with quotations and invoices, as well as having them available on the website when I create one.

I've been reading a bit recently about how to attract the attention of buyers. There seems to be a lot of support for sending a sample. I know from experience, that persistence is important because buyers tend to move around within the same company and emails can go astray. Also, timing can be crucial if you want to get a product into a supermarket for example, due to the limited number of category reviews they perform each year. These can be limited to once or twice per annum, when they rebuild their sections and decide what new products to offer, what space they need, what to drop etc.

Buyers obviously attend lots of exhibitions so this would be a good place to bump into some. Although I've exhibited at two in the past, a better option for me this time could be to get in touch with last year's exhibitors and find out whether they plan to do the next show. If the answer is yes, I could ask them to add my product to their stand and sell it for me on commission.

Buyers usually want information on current sales and market share. This probably means the company will need to have been trading for at least 12 months before making an approach to one of the chains, unless, of course, I can get them to trial it in a few stores initially because they want to be first. A one-year exclusive deal might swing it although I hear that this isn't really recommended.

I once got a foot in the door of a hotel chain but was blocked by one of the managers who stated that if they were going to buy the product that I was offering, they would be buying it from 'such and such' a firm. This was not the only time I was blocked by a company having entered some form of 'Exclusivity Agreement' with a supplier.

Sometimes if a buyer is interested, they'll give you the name of an existing supplier so that they don't have to set up an account for just one item. That means selling to the middleman, which cuts into profits; but as they're likely to know the type of items their buyers are looking for and because of the buyer referral, there's a good chance they may do a deal.

The recommended approach seems to be to send a brief email with an overview of the product concept, its unique selling points, target audience and suggested retail and cost price. It's probably a good idea to follow up with a sample. Then call them soon after. I've done something along these lines in the past and everything started off well, but only because the invention was a vast improvement on an existing product.

I've just pulled out an old business plan from 2006. It has reminded me that news releases for magazines and newspapers are a good way to get some publicity.

Registering for VAT is now top of my agenda because I want to reclaim it from my start-up costs. First, I need to find my SIC Code (75) As I've forgotten what this is I've had to look it up. I'm now able to select my type of business and product from the list. Now back to VAT registration to put the code into the appropriate box. As I've opened a bank account, I'm able to enter those details too and the form is complete.

Wednesday 5th April

I'm in the process of setting up a PayPal account today and shall need to integrate this with eBay and my e-commerce website, when I set one up. Now the website won't accept my debit card data, probably because I haven't made a deposit to activate the account yet. So, I need to get back to the bank.

I've just found an email from 'Government Gateway' which is the entry portal for access to

all the government online services. I now need to wait about a week for the activation code to come through via snail mail. (For information on the new website click here. Accessing HMRC online services using GOV.UK One Login - GOV.UK (76)

Next email confirms receipt by HMRC of my VAT registration form.

Thursday 6th April

I've just found an apprenticeship scheme for those who want to train in the craft sector worth up to £6,000 p.a. at Quest (77). Click on 'Stories' for information.

Friday 7th April

I've started work on the pricing again and I'm also creating an X account. Payment per order on eBay and X for publicity, seems the way to keep within budget.

I'm not going to be able to sell to the Pharmacy sector, until I've found a supplier able to provide tooling and injection moulding services, because any orders are likely to be on the large side.

I'm getting a little impatient for the first prototypes, so have written to the designer to place an order for 50 units. This time I've written from the company. Hopefully this will get the ball rolling and get my order into the queue.

Monday 10th April

I've always been under the impression that Superdrug is owned by Boots, but I haven't come across the name in my research, so I'll check Wikipedia (78). OK, so they are competitors, with their HQ located in Hong Kong and their registered office in the Cayman Islands. They have 800 stores across the UK and Irish Republic.

Still faffing about trying to set up online banking so I can get the reference number (code) which PayPal has sent to me. This will appear on my bank statement against a one pence inward payment. I can then activate the eBay account by entering the code.

I've been looking at Coast to Capital - Equity Growth Fund (79). Most, if not all fund holders seem to require matched funding from another source. They could for example, invest £50,000 -

£200,000, so the minimum matched funding would be £50,000. It also says that they don't require security, but if matched funding comes from a bank, I'm sure the bank would at least insist on a 'personal guarantee'. This would put everything the borrower owns at risk and would not be limited to the company assets. Matched funding from a sale of equity would seem to be a much safer bet.

I recently heard about an organization that I thought might be interesting. As an alternative to borrowing from a bank it seems possible to borrow instead from a group of 'investors', pay interest on the loan and repay the debt over time (so 'investors', in this case do not take equity in the company). But as usual I'm concerned about 'personal guarantees' so did a search of their website. I continue to be concerned that loans are offered as being unsecured when in fact they are not unsecured because if you give a personal guarantee or use a guarantor then the debt is secured against your/their personal assets and having limited company status will not save anyone in such a case. Always read the Legal Terms and Conditions in full! You must repay a loan and will not be let off. The only route may be to file for bankruptcy. An unsecured loan is one that is not secured against a business asset/s which in the event of default can be sold to repay the company debts. Lenders lend to make themselves money. They invest in the hope that you will work hard to make them more money.

I must remember that *Basepoint (80)* ***offers start-up facilities in more than 30 locations where it's possible to rent a small commercial unit for an indefinite period and need not be tied to a fixed term contract.*** Typically, they will have a number of small industrial units together with offices and meeting rooms.

Here's another potential source of finance from a fund holder called *Coast to Capital – Regional Growth Grant (81).* But again the applicant will need to find money from another source, 60% this time; but a grant is definitely preferable to a loan. I seem to recall that factoring doesn't count, because the grant or loan provider needs to see how all the funds will be used and by when; factoring is linked to future sales which are not guaranteed.

I once presented to a room full of what I thought were potential investors and would never do it again without having a glass of water close to my hand. I recently learned that the first thing to shut down when you're under stress is the digestion and as that starts in the mouth, saliva is the first to go. I wish I'd known this, because at that particular event, I could barely speak. I was perfectly confident that I knew my presentation inside out, but facing a room full of strangers made a surprising amount of difference. Also, I later discovered that a lot of the audience was made up of other entrepreneurs rather than Business Angels, so if I ever get involved with something like this in the future, I'll ask beforehand what the ratio is going to be, before parting with any money to the event managers.

My plan now is to stay small initially, keep control and contract work out.

Tuesday 11th April

My primary manufacturer has just offered me 30 days credit on their invoices, which is very helpful. This is an unusual offer to a company with no credit history.

I need to have my business plan ready soon so that I can request a factoring facility from the bank's Commercial Finance Division. I'll base my sales projections on selling to two major retail sectors.

Friday 14th April

Yesterday I received a quote from the printers for the in-store card to which I shall attach my gadgets. It came in at £285 + VAT @ 20% = £57, £342/1,000 = 0.342p each. This will include the manufacture of a shape cutter with euro-slot and artwork (at £30), so it's probably fair enough.

This quote may be a bit on the high side so I'm looking for a second quote from a competitor. I've just found another firm locally and am sending some details across to them.

During my hunt for an alternative printer, I did a quick search on my current supplier, but it seems they're trading as an unregistered entity. This is nothing unusual, but I would expect larger companies to be registered with their accounts available online.

I've now received a quote from the other printing firm which was very fast. However, it's much higher than the first, so I'll stay put for the time being and be thankful. I've asked for a pro-forma invoice because I don't want to be left with the option to pay later as I may not be able to resist or have the cash available.

It's been mentioned that different companies like to have the euro-slot standardised.

Saturday 15th April

I'm useless at mathematics, especially percentages and fractions, so always need to treat my calculations with great caution. I've now prepared two mnemonics, to help me remember the difference between Mark-Up % and Gross Profit Margin % which are easily confused and are necessary for the business plan.

To get some idea of the mark-up that retailers will expect I've carried out another 'search' and found some excellent answers. On average it seems that retailers will multiply the wholesale cost price by 2.4 which means that an item costing £1.00 will retail in store at £2.40. This will break down into £1.00 cost price, £1.00 mark-up, 40p VAT – because VAT is currently 20p in the pound. Mark-ups also seem to depend on certain criteria such as product size, anticipated speed of turnover, in store promotions being offered or even sale or return. (Written retrospectively as it's not very easy to find this sort of information). Since I've only been offering buyers a 100% mark-up, (x2) this could have made a significant difference, however, this is not necessarily a bad thing. This is a useful calculator (82).

It's important to remember that my Mark-Up is not the same as my Gross Profit (GP) or Gross Profit Margin (GPM). The former is what I shall be adding to my cost price in order to make a profit. I was once informed by a garden centre buyer that they multiply the price they buy in at by 2.5. So, if, for example, I wanted to sell my product to them at a wholesale price of £4.00; £4.00 x 2.5 would mean that they would sell it at an RRP of £10.00.

Sunday 16th April

I've just put the Mark-Up% and Gross Profit Margin% formulae into my Excel spreadsheets.

Now I can see the effect of any changes I need to make to pricing or the recommended retail price (RRP).

Wednesday 18th April

I've been thinking about using Basepoint again. Many years ago, I was offered a ground floor workshop for £1,050 per month excluding VAT. This price included buildings insurance, heating, waste disposal, on-site management, service charge and external repairs. It was a very flexible arrangement which worked on a rolling license with a 'minimum stay agreement' of one month with only 2 weeks' notice required to vacate. There is 24-hour access, free customer parking, a networking lounge etc. Naturally there's office space as well, but I didn't inquire about that.

Friday 21st April

It seems that one of the email addresses I've been using is being blocked by something called SORBS. It seems SORBS stands for 'spam and open relay blocking system' so I'll just have to find another address and try that. I must wonder whether I'm being blocked; perhaps because the supplier went to a lot of trouble quoting for something slightly complicated and I didn't follow-up. Even so, it's rather odd.

I've now received a pdf file showing the logo, so I'll sign it off and give the go ahead once I've approved the physical item. When I receive the 50 units, I'll send one to an injection moulding firm and ask for their tooling and unit prices. I'll also ask for the lead time so that I'll know how long it will take overall.

Now I've received an email from eBay which tells me that if I'm a VAT registered business I can pay eBay 'selling fees' exclusive of VAT by adding the VAT number to my account. As the VAT number hasn't come through yet it will just have to wait. I think there are different rules for business sellers and individuals who only sell infrequently on eBay. (You will need to double check).

Sunday 23rd April

I've started updating my knowledge on supply chain management and have been watching some YouTube videos on procurement.

Wednesday 26th April

I should have received my VAT number by now. I'm supposed to access customer communications from the 'Your HMRC Services' page, to see if they've sent me the registration number, but naturally I can't find the link anywhere.

I've had a browse on the HMRC website and can see that I'm eligible to use their ***VAT Cash Accounting Scheme (83).*** This entitles me to pay VAT on my sales when my customers pay me and reclaim VAT on my purchases when I've paid my supplier. It is very important to check this by visiting the HMRC website!

Thursday 27th April

Using the ***Freedom of Information Act (84), I'm going to try and find out a couple of things.***

Saturday 29th April

I'm calculating that if the UK population is 65,000,000 and I project sales of 364,000 units by the end of year three, or 121,333 per annum; 364,000/65,000,000 = 0.006×100 = 0.6% of the population being targeted over a period of 3 years. But as only about half the population might need the product, I'm going to divide 65,000,000/2 and get 32,500,000 as my potential market size.

So, 364,000 as a percentage of 32,500,000 would be 364,000/32,500,000 = 0.01×100 = 1.10%. Therefore, over the first three years of trading I expect to target 1.10% or 364,000 of half the UK population.

Please note: ***When you see a padlock icon next to a website name in the browser, it is supposed to indicate that the website is secured with a digital certificate and any information sent between your browser and the website is sent securely and cannot be intercepted and read by someone else while in transit.*** However, this may not always be the case so please use your own judgment.

MAY

Tuesday 2nd May

I'm looking for exhibition centres where I can exhibit or talk to potential buyers. ExCeL has nothing suitable at present.

Wednesday 3rd May

With old business plans scattered throughout the house, I've come across some information on maximising publicity by entering competitions. These seem to include Banks' National Business Awards and SME Regional Business Awards just for starters which I should consider in due course.

Friday 5th May

Against my better judgment, I've now placed an order with the printer for 1,000 promotional leaflets. I want to have something finished to show buyers and hand out, but it's an expensive way to do this.

I'm looking at Factoring and Invoice Discounting again and have found a lot more information. The difference between the two is that with factoring, the finance provider manages the sales ledger and performs the credit control function, chasing customers for settlement of invoices. With invoice discounting, I would perform this function myself and the customer doesn't need to know that I'm using the facility.

Saturday 6th May

I want to get online banking sorted out now so I can pay my suppliers conveniently.

Sunday 7th May

I've been investigating IP Insurance once more and there's a lot of information on the IPO website with appropriate links. I've just added the following under the Intellectual Property section of my business plan. "Intellectual Property Insurance has been discussed with (named) Insurance Company and will be activated simultaneously with invoice discounting and business insurance. This will be as soon as the company invoices its first major order". I've now sent an email to the IP insurance broker asking him to email some information to me.

On the topic of invoicing, the HMRC website states clearly what information must be included

on an invoice here (85) and some rules are set out on their next page here (86).

Monday 8th May

On or about the 14th May I shall be able to add the Registered Trademark symbol ® after my brand name. It's illegal to use this until the trademark has been granted registered status.

Now I need to order some more product. I've designed a company order template myself, but I think Microsoft Office (which I've now purchased) has a comprehensive range which I shall investigate in due course.

Thursday 11th May

Up bright and early and I've just received a call from the IP Insurance Broker. Basically, what I require is Legal Expenses Insurance to (1) defend against the allegation that I've infringed on another person/firms' intellectual property and (2) to pursue any entity that in my opinion is infringing on my IP. I've explained that I'm very loan averse and that I'm using invoice finance to help with cash flow; therefore, I would not wish to activate cover, or pay for this, until I've invoiced my first order. The broker said that this was not a problem and just to call him when ready. Also, on the issue of the IP being registered with the IPO in my name, I should just notify him when this is licensed exclusively to my company. Quotes from the Insurance Company are only valid for 30 days, after which he will have to get an update if I need one. The fact that this is a UK patent only was discussed, the USA being much more expensive due to their fondness for litigation.

I've suddenly decided to register the design. This is because I'm suffering from a dose of inventor paranoia today. The more involved I get with the business plan and can visualize the potential profit, the more anxious I get that someone will take advantage or challenge my IP. After all my hard work, this would be heart breaking.

Friday 12th May

I contacted 3D Co. today, to ask for more information about the release fee for the data files and drawings that they've produced for me. These, like photographs remain their property, unless they've been bought outright. Their response was along the lines that any release fee was at their discretion and was usually reserved for higher value projects where they have spent many hours on a design. In my case there would be no charge, and they hold no ownership of my designs. My order was now at the front of the queue and would be polished and shipped by Tuesday. This is good news, however, because I'm commercialising the item, I think it would be wise to get the MD or another authorized signatory, to sign something to this effect, so that I can register the design and not discover later that a question of ownership of the IP has arisen.

Wednesday 17th May

I mustn't forget to do a 'What if? / Sensitivity Analysis' for the business plan. This analyses what would happen if sales were to drop by a certain percentage, leaving me unable to pay my 'overheads' aka 'fixed costs'.

One way to introduce the product would be to offer it to a shopping channel, but this isn't a route I want to go down. As I understand it, they would place an order for many items which I would have to finance, on a 'sale or return' basis. This cannot be factored. Delivery would be to their warehouse on pallets and payment would be received in due course. As this would be an opening gambit on an unproven product, and I'd need to take out a loan or sell equity to raise the funds for stock production, it would be an extremely high-risk strategy at such an early stage. Then if it didn't sell as well as expected, I'd have to refund the outstanding balance and retrieve the goods. I could end up holding a lot of unsold stock and need to continue paying interest to the bank on a loan. Storing the goods might also be a headache. There may be slight differences between shopping channels, but this is the general gist of how I believe it works.

Unsolicited calls from overseas companies representing themselves as TV shopping channels, will also be treated with caution as will any direct sales approaches being made to the company from an uncheckable source. I've recently learned that there is something called an 'Infomercial' whereby the channel sells your product on TV for a fee.

I'm still waiting for a response to my Freedom of Information Request.

Thursday 18th May

I've now written to an injection moulding firm to ask them to quote for tooling and parts.

Friday 19th May

I received an email from 3D Co. today, saying that they've started work on my job and I'll receive the artwork proof next Monday, at the very latest.

I was once given the opportunity by an injection moulding firm, to spread the cost of the tooling (amortize it) over a two-year period. A small percentage of the cost was going to be added to the price of each moulded unit, to pay off the debt.

Saturday 20th May

I've been up since 7 o'clock emailing my Patent Agent. I just wanted to clarify a few things, before completing the application for IP insurance. As I've drafted the patent application myself without help, there's something I need to ask about which, if I'm lucky, I shall get a response to without dipping into my non-existent resources. When I said without help, I should add that 'Patent Examiners' who deal with applications at the

Patent Office, are always very thorough in their critique of the applicant's wording and are as helpful as possible. Also, the IPO has an officer, who will happily answer questions about independent application procedures, wording etc. over the phone.

Some years ago, when I was clueless, I was introduced to the inventor of a well-known home improvement product and invited to his home. He was extremely pleasant and helpful. He mentioned that he'd been granted a further patent on an unrelated item which had been infringed, but was having to take legal action in person, due to the very high legal costs. Even so, this must have been expensive, especially if he failed to win. I was also introduced to an ex-patent examiner, who was doing voluntary work to help small businesses. So, there's help out there without it costing a fortune.

Monday 22nd May

This morning, I went to visit my local Paydens to see where they might hang the product if it were chosen by the buyer. I've discovered that they don't have a specific section for this category at all. However, I thought it might go next to a similar but unconnected product range hung on pegs, with a green and white theme. The chemist is located close to Tesco, so should be quite busy. I think Tesco Extra have a Pharmacy section which is worth remembering and I seem to recall that the Lloyds brand, is now associated with more than 200 Sainsbury's in-store pharmacies.

I've just been to check out an independent pharmacy and was shocked to see that they use a single prong from which to hang goods. Although I indicated to the printer that I needed a euro-slot, I had not specified that it needed to have a hemi-sphere at the top. Without this any product would slip to one side.

Saturday 27th May

Yesterday I was struggling to remember how to do a 'Break-Even Analysis'. This should tell me how many units I need to sell, to cover my 'Total Fixed Costs' (overheads) i.e. salaries, rent, accounting fees, insurance etc. so that I can start to make a profit. (1) I will look for my spreadsheets and locate my 'Cash Flow Forecast' first, then look for the 'Total Fixed Costs' (overheads) figure which is a sub-total near the bottom, on the right-hand side, (let's say it's £50,000). (2) I will look for my 'Variable Cost Price' per unit. This figure I will find in a table that I've prepared and headed 'Pricing Breakdown', which will also end up in the Business Plan. The table shows how I've added up all the separate parts that go to make up one unit. I've taken into account the cost of the individual items, the packaging, assembly and dispatch services which will vary from time to time, as my 'suppliers' in turn are affected by their own variable costs such as wages directly linked to production, the cost of raw materials, transport etc. and pass on the cost of any increase to their customers. Let's say the variable cost price is £5.00. (3) Let's say I have decided to sell each unit at a wholesale 'selling price' of £8.00 (ex. VAT) this would give me a mark-up of 60% (i.e. balance/cost price = 60 x 100 = 60%) so my equation would be as follows:

Total Fixed Costs (Overheads) £50,000

Selling price £8.00 Less Variable Cost £5.00 per unit = £3.00

Calculate: £50,000 / £3.00

I must therefore sell 16,666 units to be able to pay all my Fixed Costs/Overheads.

This equation really focuses the mind, and I need to scrutinize all my overheads very carefully, to see whether they are essential during this start-up phase. Selling 16,666 units, (for example) before I even start to make a profit would be horrendous, so I must cut my fixed costs to the bone wherever possible. I should also be on the alert for any free advertising opportunities.

I visited the printers today and I must say that I'm really impressed by their work. They chose a good quality card, added colour and shaping then very strategically placed the necessary holes. I chose a pale green which seems to be popular with pharmacies, so that adding a new product will not jar with the existing display. All this needed a bit of face-to-face contact.

I've just received a very positive response to a question I directed to the examiner at the IPO who dealt with my patent application. It was probably a bit of a cheek to ask for his advice at this stage, but I've always found examiners to be very kind and helpful, so my advice to anyone would be just to keep plugging away, if you're making an application as an individual, and when they respond with a question or objection, never see it as a negative but an opportunity to work out why they should grant you a patent and respond. I found that I had the most difficulty with the claims.

Sunday 28th May

This break-even calculation is quite wonderful. I'm now visiting my Cash Flow Forecast and highlighting the 'projected unit sales' figures, taken from my 'Sales Projections' spreadsheet, (which I chose to put at the very top) in pink, before the break-even point. Then I've highlighted the 'projected unit sales' figures after the break-even point in green. I can now see the wisdom of delaying some purchases and therefore won't be placing any orders for tooling, for the injection moulded parts, until after I break even in month nine. Unless I'm mistaken, tooling costs should be entered in the appropriate month, beneath the 'Total Overheads' figure against 'Capital Equipment', with the VAT owed to

HMRC and Corporation Tax below this. This is how I do it anyway.

I've now added a note at the top of my 'Notes to the Cash Flow' headed 'Break-even Point': "We expect to break even at the end of month (whatever), when the total anticipated profit on sales exceeds the total sum of the overheads for the whole year"; (except that I'm using my own figures, not those in the example).

My choice of headings for the Cash Flow Forecast now looks like this. Unit Sales; Sales (revenue); VAT on sales; Total sales incl. VAT; Invoice Discounting (sub heading); 80% of total invoice value; Balance of 20% on invoice; Total factored receipts (incl. VAT); Payments (variable costs); VAT on payments; Total Payments incl. VAT; Gross Profit; GP Margin %; Overheads (sub heading); Petty cash & office expenses; Rent, rates and amenities; Insurance IP/Business/Goods; Salary; Vehicle/fuel/service/tax/insurance; IT; Promotion/advertising; Accountancy/book-keeping; Legal/Professional Fees; Bank Interest & Charges (includes invoice discounting fees); Total Overheads; Pre-tax Profit/(Loss); Capital

Expenditure; VAT payable; Corporation Tax; Net surplus/(deficit); Cumulative surplus/(deficit).

Now the 'Cash Flow Forecast' looks very different and provides much needed clarity. I'm going to cut all the fixed costs to the barest minimum, not advertise and will confine my marketing effort to news releases, X and Instagram, until after the break-even point.

I've switched my attention to the matter of IP insurance (87) once again, before deciding what type of cover I need and before completing the application form, sent by the Insurance Broker a few weeks ago. I'll get them to include the trademark as well as the patent for insurance purposes, because it's important. I've just looked online to see whether it's been registered yet. It's now the 28th of May and it's supposed to take 2 months so must be imminent.

Monday 29th May

I've been doing some more reading about business insurance. It seems that I probably need 'transit insurance' but can check with the firm I've chosen to provide assembly and distribution services first as I think they're bound to have this type of cover.

I've responded to the Injection Moulding Firm's request for drawings and sent them the ones provided by the 3D Company, which I've been assured belong to me. However, because of some blurb in their Terms & Conditions, I've asked them to invoice me for £25, as I think that some form of consideration (money in this case) is required to validate the contract. Anyway, I've taken their earlier assurances to heart and sent the drawings, as I need a quote for the moulding tool and a unit price.

The IP insurance application form asks whether I have certain clauses contained in my Terms of Contract, which I guess are the Terms & Conditions of Sale. So, I'm going to copy the T&Cs from an online supplier and then include the required clauses. Unless I do this, I shan't be able to send off the form.

Tuesday 30th May

I'm trying to find templates for Terms and Conditions of Sale Agreements, because the ones

I was interested in copying don't go far enough. As these are legally binding on both parties, they're extremely important to get right. So, I've just 'searched' how to write Terms & Conditions and found some useful bits and pieces.

I've been thinking about some of the start-up stories that I've heard over the years of which this is one

Two Business Advisors once took some inventors to visit an injection moulding firm. They asked the company's management, whether they would be willing to amortize the tooling costs, in return for the business. They were turned down. However, the firm was manufacturing goods for a well-known brand and suggested that they provide an introduction, with a view to a Licensing arrangement. But these chaps were so keen to keep what they saw as a brilliant business opportunity for themselves, that they wouldn't consider it; understandably, they wanted to stop working for other people and build their own little empire. With hindsight, they thought that they should probably have had at least one meeting to find out more, as they obviously missed out on some very valuable feedback! It turned out that licensing would have been perfect, as it became a massive undertaking to get their product to market. But in their defence, they were full of enthusiasm, and it was probably too soon for them to give up their ambitions for the company they'd put so much energy into starting up. Unfortunately, they never did get their invention to market.

I've just found a 'Trademark Tracker' link on the IPO website. All I need to do, is type in my email and password and they'll send me a link. Then I can search for trademarks and their stage of progress. I've reached a page with a lot of tick boxes, so I've just ticked one which says to 'email me' when my trademark has been granted registered status.

Wednesday 31st May

This morning, I decided I should be able to find some information on copyright protection. The reason I'm so interested in copyright now, is that I want to use a slogan to promote my product. According to my research on the IPO website, items that can be protected are 'art, films, TV, web content, sound recordings, writing and literary works and photography'. This would seem to support my view, that I should have the design rights assigned by the 3D company to my own business.

The 3D Company has now assigned a whole parcel of design work, which can be used by injection moulding firms to mass produce the parts. This was definitely the right action to take. The IPO material also confirms in so many words, that all designs set out in my patent applications, are protected by unregistered design right for 15 years

I've found some interesting resources, workshops, events and webinars on the British Library website (88). However, following a cyber-attack, electronic resources such as Mintel are currently unavailable.

Regarding the use of a slogan, I've discovered that phrases or names are not protected under copyright law in the UK. Nor are slogans or titles, so I'm unlikely to be sued for using the one I like.

On a different page about 'copyright notification' I discovered that I should put the year after the

symbol as in Copyright © 2022 followed by the company name.

Another question in my mind concerns getting the small independent buyers to agree to my 'terms and conditions of sale'. It seems to be the usual practice for order pads (the company printed ones) to have terms written on the back of the order form in small print, so that by signing the order, customers are agreeing to the terms of sale. Naturally, as most orders are now placed electronically, the T & Cs will be attached.

I just went into email to chase up the IPO but am having problems with my service provider. I'm getting pop-up messages saying that my email can't be sent; so, I've had to take a screenshot of this so I can send it to their support team. I did this by pressing 'Print Screen' (top right) then typed 'Paint' into the 'search box', (bottom left). Once in 'Paint' I pressed 'Control V'; clicked on 'Crop' to cut out the private bits and then 'Delete'. I've now sent a copy of this edited photo from my private account - the one from which I signed up with my ISP - and asked for help. Just to clarify I have been using the same Internet Service Provider

(ISP) for years and they provide my email and website services.

I'm trying to discover how long a large retail customer would normally take to pay their suppliers and find myself here (89) ***on the GOV.UK website again***. I once heard that it was quite normal for invoices to be paid by the larger firms at the end of the month following receipt of the supplier's invoice. So, if my terms of payment are 30 days, it won't help me much if I'm only given 30 days' credit by my suppliers but won't get paid for something like 50 - 60 days. It was once suggested that I try to deliver goods and the invoice towards the end of the month; to reduce the time I would be waiting for payment. However, this is where I need to factor initially, arrange an overdraft perhaps, or start negotiating hard with my suppliers for longer to pay. For example, for the period March 1st – August 31st one company paid 74% of their customers within 30 days, 21% within 60 days and 5% in more than 60 days.

As this book is obviously about the World of Work, you might want to consider a career in the

Armed Forces so I've included links to the British Army (90), Royal Navy (91), and the Royal Air Force (92)

JUNE

Friday 2nd June

I've now paid my first manufacturer's invoice which was simple with online banking. They seem to be using the same Commercial Finance firm that I hope to use. I sent the money to the 'factor' as requested on their invoice and now need to send a 'remittance advice' to let them know that the invoice has been paid. I did a 'search' to see what I could discover about remittance by BACS (Bankers' Automated Clearing Services) and it says to include the BACS reference. I'm not sure what this is so I've just put whose bill I'm paying as the reference and will look for more information later. The transaction has not immediately shown up on my bank statement, so I'll check in a few days and send off the remittance advice when the money has gone.

I emailed the intellectual property Insurance Agent, to ask about the 'confidentiality clause' which the insurers expect to be included in my T&Cs. He responded along the lines that not all of them want it included. In fact, I can see that such clauses are not even relevant to my IP protection, because everything about my product has already been published.

I've just discovered a perfect set of T&Cs that I can copy. The general advice is that they should go on the rear of all contractual documents. Order Forms, Quotes, Delivery Notes, Acknowledgment of Order Forms, in catalogues and on websites.

Following my email to the IPO, I'm told that my trademark application will go to Registration on the 9th of July.

The IP Insurance Application form has a lot of questions requiring a bit of thought. They ask what 'risk management' procedures I have in place for protecting the IP, so I've put the following. "On the last day of each month, the CEO will carry out online searches to identify any product that might be infringing the patent and check the 'Patents and TM Journals'. The company will also be making a Registered Design application". It's not a lot but I expect it will do. The next question relates to discovery of an infringement? My answer is "I would immediately contact the Insurer first and then speak to the company's Patent Agent for further advice". Next, a question about my crisis management procedures: So I've put "In the event of any serious complaint or injury arising as a result of the use of the product, the company will, (a) inform the insurance company, (b) request advice from the insurance company and act in the appropriate manner, which could be to contact all retail store buyers and ask that they follow their usual recall procedures and (c) contact the company's Patent Agent". Now I must create a digital signature. I need help with this.

Sunday 4th June

I've finally signed up for a basic Website package for £1.00 per month for one year increasing to £11.99 thereafter. When I tried to set the website up just now, I received a message saying, "Your product cannot be edited because 'Private Browsing' mode is enabled on your browser". I've no idea how to disable it and I also need assistance with the online digital signature.

I really must register the design to be on the safe side. It seems to cost £50 for online registration and £60 by snail mail. I think I can manage this, as I'm doing the VAT return at the end of the month and shall be able to recoup about £100. It appears that protection lasts for up to 25 years but must be renewed every five. I shall include the patent and registered design numbers in any correspondence with injection moulding firms.

I've been struggling to find an appropriate template for the website and have just found one showing lots of happy young people with their hands in the air. I like this, so I'm going to use it and put my slogan at the top.

I seem to have misunderstood the process of paying by BACS so had to go back into the bank account. What I'd done was set up the details for a payee (the 'factor') but had forgotten to enter the amount, so I needed to click on the payee and add the sum. I can now advise the factoring company that the bill's been paid.

Today I received a very positive response to the question I posed to my Patent Agent, and all seems well. Having a contact in the profession really helps but if you haven't one, first consultations are usually free and last about fifteen minutes.

I've just gone digital and have now got a signature on the application form. The stumbling block was that I didn't understand the jargon, whether something should be high or low; so high was chosen and when I clicked on 'sign', it came up with the name of the document. I was signing the 'document', so clicked on 'Save' and the job was done.

I want to add a registered design to the insurance cover but haven't registered it yet. According to the IPO website, I need drawings without any measurements indicated. After a few attempts and a bit of cutting out, I've managed to get something onto a sheet of A4 that I'm going to scan into 'My Documents'.

It's a nightmare. I can't find out how to save the scanned image now. I'm in something called 'My Image Garden'. I'm going to try this in 'Fax and Scan' – no luck again. I've now clicked on 'Settings' and it seems that I can set up how I want the document to be scanned, the document name etc. It will then be saved in 'Documents'. OK. Now I just need to click on 'Settings' again and give it a name.

So far so good. Now to try and send the application form to the IPO. The first thing I notice, is that I'm not permitted to upload a pdf which is what my drawings are saved in, so I need to find out how to change them from pdf format to TIFF, GIF or JPEG. I think I will try 'search'. I've looked through all the download services and have decided to send the document by snail mail 'special delivery' instead, so it should arrive tomorrow. Better safe than sorry. This is the link I'm looking at for details about how to Register (93)

I've now found the online application form, but it comes at the end – following a letter. I've filled it out and printed off 2 copies. I also need to print off the fee sheet and enclose a cheque for £60. The fee sheet is here (94).

When filling out the IPO 'fee sheet' the Form type and number is the one at the bottom right-hand corner; for designs it's DF2A. Now I can't find the cheque book, so I'm going to try and pay online. Sending payment before the forms seems a bit odd, but perhaps it will work. Yes, it seems fine, I can pay by debit card, so I'll click on the link. Now that's done I'm going to finish the fee sheet. I've typed the number given to me in the 'acknowledgment of payment' on Form FS2. I'm clipping them all together now, the designs, the fee sheet FS2 and the application to Register a Design Form DF2A.

So, I've applied to register the design and am now waiting for the acknowledgment and a number which should come by email. When it arrives, I can put it into the IP insurance application with a note that an application to register the design has been made. Then send the insurance application form to the Agent, who will send it to various insurers. I'm told that not too many offer IP insurance, but I should receive an offer quite soon.

Tuesday 6th June

I've just sent an email off (the 'Remittance Advice') to my supplier's factor, so that they're aware that the bill has been paid. I only put the name of the supplier, the amount and the invoice number, so I hope that's all they required.

Thursday 8th June

I'm reading an example of some Terms and Conditions (T&Cs) and have come across the term SKU which stands for stock-keeping unit. The following US website provides some very clear information on SKUs (95) which I must read in full later.

Sunday 9th June

Regarding obtaining IP insurance. If I decide to accept an offer, then I shall need to type up a 'Resolution' (a legally binding decision), resolving that my company has agreed to enter into an agreement with an individual (myself), to purchase either by way of a transfer, or an exclusive licensing agreement, all intellectual property currently owned by me for a consideration of … whatever. I must then file an IPO 'Notice of Rights' form (96) showing change of ownership and pay the relevant fee, which is currently £50. This is because it's the intellectual property belonging to the company that the insurers will be insuring.

While looking for information on licensing of intellectual property, I found a Skeleton License

on the IPO website showing the major issues to consider and the types of clauses one might find in a Licensing Agreement (97).

I received a phone call this morning from the insurance broker. For product liability insurance it will cost the company between 1.5K and 2.5K per year.

I've received a quotation from the Injection Moulding firm and the cost of manufacturing the tool would be £12,500 plus VAT of £2,500. This is because I want the work done in the UK to support British business. I shall therefore be better off using 3D Co. until I've passed the break-even point.

Sunday 11th June

I've just asked myself the hypothetical question "what happens if the company has to be liquidated?" The term 'reversionary clause' springs to mind, so I did a 'search'. It seems the reversionary clause should say something along the lines of '...if at any stage the company should prove unsustainable or enter into liquidation etc. the Assignment will automatically become null, and void and the intellectual property shall revert in its entirety to the Assignor' (me) … and so on.

I've also been reminded that I should be doing a SWOT analysis for the business. This stands for strengths, weaknesses, opportunities and threats.

Monday 12th June

I've now found some information about assigning a UK patent *here (98)* but can't find much else.

Tuesday 13th June

I have a horrible feeling that I've been hugely over-optimistic. My final job last night was to carry out a 'What If Analysis' to see whether the business could survive if my projections were to vary by ten or twenty percent, based on my Profit & Loss forecast. If I can't meet my financial commitments, then I'll probably have to start borrowing or sell equity if a buyer can be found. There are lots of videos on YouTube to help with this analysis. A bank loan with a personal guarantee would be the worst scenario because then I'd be putting everything I own at risk. Maintaining the wholesale selling price in the face of buyer pressure is key to staying afloat, along with finding new customers and making a profit.

I under-estimated the unit cost of each item produced by the injection moulding process so I'm going to look for another supplier.

Wednesday 14th June

I've just ordered some visiting cards online, because it would be daft to visit a potential customer and not leave one.

The jiffy bags have arrived. I chose something large enough for the product with its store-card attached and checked with the post office what it would cost. The lady managed to drag it through the measuring slot so that it would be less than £2.50 to post, but I doubt everyone will be that determined, or goodhearted. (This turned out to be very true).

This morning, I started to consider an overdraft facility. So, I searched online and discovered that the current 'arrangement fee' with my bank for an overdraft facility, is 1.5% on the total borrowing limit; or for a small amount it would be a minimum charge of £100. Since I only want

£1,000 for the moment, this is too expensive, not to mention the fact that the company would be carrying a debt. I'm going to have to work around this.

Wednesday 21st June

The business cards have cost me £13.32 for a standard business card, shipping £3.99 (VAT £3.47) making a total of £17.31 ex. VAT. So, each card will cost £0.7p as I've only ordered 250 but the unit cost would have been cheaper had I bought more.

I've set up the website under the company name.com, but I also need to get the .co.uk address pointing towards it, so that people can type in either IP address to get there.

Sunday 25th June

My internet service provider (ISP) has been on the phone helping me to transfer my .com domain name, to my Basic Website package/contract. I haven't completed the feedback form yet, as I'm waiting to see if I've been charged. (I was, but not a lot).

Now I need to 'point' my .co.uk domain towards my domain name .com, so that anyone typing in the former will arrive at the .com website. 'Forwarding a domain' allows you to redirect your visitors to another website. This can be done using 'framing', when the visitor will not see any change take place; but the way I'm going to do it which seems to be simpler, allows the visitor to see in the address bar that the .co.uk domain name has changed to .com.

Monday 26th June

Another thought which has just sprung to mind, is that buyers will expect a quantity discount, just as I do myself. So, I've put up the wholesale price by £1.00 so that I can produce a price list for 50, 500, 1,000, 5,000 and 10,000, decreasing the cost by £0.25 increments, until I arrive at the price I've been quoting in my cash flow projections.

I must remember to send a sample of the product to Better Pathways whose employees are able to gain work experience while suffering from mental health issues.

Wednesday 28th June

I seem to be having one disaster after another on this computer. First, I was unable to get into any of my documents – it felt as if somebody else was controlling them – and just now when I came to edit the diary, everything went haywire. I was told that I couldn't get in, because 'info' had blocked it, and I could only open it in 'Read only' mode.

JULY

Saturday 1st July

I received a quote from the IP insurance company yesterday and the price is £3,500 for £500,000 of protection, so it's on hold for the moment.

I've updated the company accounts so that I can reclaim the VAT that I've paid out so far. I'll be getting a rebate soon which will help with cash flow a little.

Wednesday 12th July

I managed to send off the Business Plan and factoring application form to the Commercial Finance Manager yesterday.

I now need to prepare some samples with 'Assembly Instructions' for my potential assembly provider so that they can give me a price. They invited me to send a Non-disclosure Agreement (NDA), so I'm now waiting to get their signed copy back.

I received the alternative tooling estimate yesterday and was really shocked to see that the work was to be done in China, so I wish I'd checked before sending the drawings. Previously, I've been given a choice of British or less expensive Chinese tooling if there was one. The lead time is quoted as 15 weeks to get everything made and tested, which is another reason I'm not keen, despite the lower price. (With hindsight I should have discussed any tooling options with this company first).

Thursday 13th July

I've just emailed a wholesale buyer in the south-east and was very surprised to receive a call within 10 minutes. She sounded very nice but said that they don't do very well with my type of product, so not to raise my hopes. She can see me on the 26th of July. My cash flow forecast shows sales starting in October, as I plan to allow eight weeks for production and delivery. An order now would be perfect.

I sent some samples off yesterday to Better Pathways (99) and have had a chat with the Manager. I hope they won't charge more than

£1.00 per unit for assembly, because that will put all my numbers out.

Wednesday 19th July

I've been checking the accounts of a small logistics firm that I was thinking of using on the Company's House website, and they seem to be borrowing on a regular basis. I had to email them first, to ask for their company number which wasn't on their website, and the name of the company was very different to their trading name.

I phoned up two more retailers that I want to email and was given the buyers' names. I'm going to wait until I've had a dry run with the South-East buyer first though, who unfortunately took the trouble to confirm by email just now, that she's genuinely not interested in my type of product. Nevertheless, I'm looking on the bright side and she will give me feedback which is extremely valuable.

I've now had a quote from** Better Pathways (100)* ***which is reasonable. Next, I need to work out how the goods will get delivered onward to my customers.

I've just emailed a chain store and offered to send them a sample. (No response – I think I should have sent one anyway).

Saturday 22nd July

I'm looking at the Entrepreneurs' Handbook now which seems rather interesting. It has among other things, a finance page here (101) which explains VAT very well and another here (102) that lists grants and loans. It also explains about the Seed Enterprise Investment Scheme which gives tax relief to investors.

I'm starting to think that I really should consider a small investment from a Business Angel. And while on this topic, another story I once heard was told to me by a different couple of chaps, not the above, who felt they'd surely dodged a bullet. They'd been introduced by the owner of an injection moulding firm to two much more experienced inventors (the middlemen), who were already working with an overseas investor on a related product. The middlemen were convinced that they could raise investment for these two from the same source, but only after 'they' had edited their business plan. In return they would receive equity of 5% each. To cut a long story short, the proposal was to offer 51% to the potential investors. They never learned who they were but acted on trust. (This doesn't seem very sensible). As the editor of the business plan neared the end of his work, the pair revealed that they'd decided not to offer 51% after all. They offered 49% instead. Even so, this would have seen them lose control because of the 10% that they'd already trustingly allotted to the middlemen, but this had rather slipped their minds at the time. It was a deal where they were being offered a buy-back option, when their fledgling company met certain targets. It was obviously their change of mind that lost the deal for them. The poor old inventors suspected they would have been working their fingers to the bone to meet target expectations, for only 19.5% each and probably gone mad. It's sometimes said that owning 100% of nothing, is still nothing but that was not the point. Unfortunately, they failed to get to market but retained their sanity which was far more important.

Wednesday 26th July

It's been a very interesting morning. I left the house at 8.30 and arrived for my first meeting with the buyer in the South-East. I had laid out my glorious new and innovative products neatly in a row inside a beautiful velvet box so that she could take the lid off and experience 'the reveal'. Sadly, my gadgets weren't quite what she expected and I'm afraid she didn't understand how they were going to help her customers. So, I performed a demonstration which went rather well I thought. She asked whether anyone else was buying now, so I had to admit that she was my first potential customer. That was more or less it, and I stood up to go. Thus, my first visit with a buyer ended after only ten minutes.

It's now two hours later and I know that the problem was of my own making due to my lack of selling skills. I wasn't expecting the objections and didn't know how to overcome them. Crucially I forgot to generate the WIFT factor (what's in it for them). It's said that people buy from people. It must have been a very odd presentation for her to experience.

I've decided to use PALL-EX for distribution. They seem to operate using a hub and depot network and recruit independent hauliers all over the country. They have a hub (just one big one) in Leicester. The haulier will collect from the pick-up location e.g. Better Pathways and take the euro-cartons (essentially euro-cartons to fit the pallets) to the PALL-EX Hub. There, they will be sorted and allocated to the appropriate haulier, who will take the goods onward to their own depot. From there, they'll be sorted and put onto small vans for delivery to their destination.

Saturday 29th July

I have a couple of computer towers sitting in my hallway now. I'm trying to work out how to kill-off the hard drives so that they can't be accessed after I take them to the dump.

The Commercial Manager to whom I applied for a factoring facility hasn't got back to me yet and will be on leave for the next two weeks. He did say however, that his checks had all come back clear and he didn't foresee any problems, so that's a positive start.

AUGUST

This is where the computer crashed without my having updated the memory stick.

SEPTEMBER

Tuesday 5th September

I'm going to edit the ad-words (meta-tags) on the website now, because it's been up for over two weeks, and I haven't seen any visitors yet. I can check the numbers by using the site's analytics function, but it seems to be very basic unless I pay for it. For £0.99 I really shouldn't complain. (Much later I discovered that I'd misunderstood the format which is to simply put a comma in between key words or after a short string of two or three words).

I placed an order for my product on eBay today, just to check how smoothly the buying process worked.

Thursday 7th September

The order that I placed on eBay seems to be running smoothly and I've received lots of auto confirmation emails from them and PayPal. I've clicked on 'dispatched' and the next message says that my order will arrive tomorrow.

I've been receiving prompt messages when I'm on eBay, saying that they no longer support Chrome 32. So, I've done a 'search' to find out how to download the latest version. There was a lot about the administrator having blocked updates on this computer, (its second hand) but in the end I simply downloaded the (presumably) latest version. So now I've got something. No idea what exactly and have given up caring.

Saturday 9th September

I'm trying to cancel a couple of website domains that I no longer need, but because I've had problems in the past, I'm typing the process here, so I won't forget. To find the 'Cancellations' section, click on 'Contracts and Product Overview', followed by the 'Domain contract/package' that I want to cancel. Under the 'My Account' section, I will find 'Cancellation' and this takes me to the correct web page.

As I no longer have a use for it, I'm trying to dissolve a company name, but the Company's House website has failed to explain adequately, how to apply for strike off (dissolution) of a company. (I now suspect that this was my failing and not theirs). So I've had to 'search' for the information, which is on the GOV.UK (103) website. It was then easy to find Form DS01 and print it off. I now need to send it by snail mail with a cheque for £10. Because I never used this company name, I haven't set up a business bank account, so it's only the name that requires cancellation.

Sunday 24th September

On Friday I was messing around for ages with the computer because the time kept re-setting itself to 1947. Even a full scan didn't clear it. So, I went to the computer store and bought another battery. I winkled out the old one, making a diagram lest I forget where to put the leads back in, but when it was all set up again, it was still 1947! Then I remembered, that on a previous occasion I'd been sold a dud battery, so went and bought one from a different shop which did the trick. I couldn't get annoyed though because the computer chap gave me some very good advice. I was shown what the 'hard drive' looked like and told how to remove it, so at last I can take the towers to the recycling centre. (I could probably have found this information on YouTube, if I'd thought to have a look).

I can see on 'site analytics' that people or robots are still looking at my website in the middle of our night. The browser looking on this occasion was called Opera which is popular in Africa and some parts of Asia apparently.

Tuesday 26th September

I've just spoken to a lady on the switchboard of a company in the southeast to whom I hope to introduce my gadget. She told me that the usual way to introduce a new product was to email their Buying Department which I'll do now.

I've just received a response from this firm inviting me to register the company on their website – there was a link in the email. It seems they want a 4% discount on all invoices, and 90 days to pay them. Furthermore, the list is long and requires details of my manufacturing facility and the name of at least one customer, or up to 4 that make up at least 10% of my customer base. Oh yes, and my company needs to be a member of SEDEX, so I'm about to 'search' for that.

SEDEX stands for Supplier Ethical Data Exchange apparently. This is a global organization, enabling suppliers to add their data to the SEDEX (104) website providing easy access to information by buyers. The company must adhere to certain ethical conditions, and it costs £60 per annum to be on there. I presume I would need to give manufacturing data from my suppliers; but would I want to reveal their names? Probably not, but I could start by asking them whether they're already a member of SEDEX. There's too much to read for now so I'll leave it until I've got some customers and then think again if I can overcome my reluctance to allowing 90 days credit. Probably not.

I really must put some money back into PayPal. I moved some – very easily – across to the company bank account and now I have a payment to make to eBay, which it seems must come out of the PayPal account. But I could be mistaken, because I think they have a fallback position in case there are insufficient funds, in which case they'll take payment from the business account, no doubt I'll discover more soon.

I now have a good photograph illustrating the product on my website. I simply placed the item on a piece of white foam-board and took my photo.

There used to be a useful business directory at my library called KOMPASS. It was in hardback and listed the names of company buyers and top management. There was also an online directory where users could search for market research, published by Mintel (105). I'm off now to see whether I can track them down.

Tuesday 27th September

I've found a rather nice little website selling an assortment of items. They had a pop-up customer service 'chat' box which was helpful. I said that I thought they might be interested in an innovative gadget, so they gave me the buyer's email. The company has just acknowledged receipt and said they would get back to me. (They never did)

The factoring manager called this morning and pointed out an irregularity in my Terms & Conditions. It seems that I haven't made it clear that invoices will only be sent out after I've received confirmation of receipt of the goods. He also mentioned that the website looked better now that I've added further information.

I'm pleased to see that my home page is coming up on 'search' now, together with some images from eBay.

I've clicked on the offer of Free SSL (secure socket layer) that my ISP is offering for the website. It seems that after one year it will cost £10.00 which seems OK, so long as it's per year and not per month. From what I can discover, this puts the website further up the list of search engines and improves security.

It's 9.10 a.m. so I've just put in a call to the head office switchboard of a major retailer in the north of England. The operator was very efficient when I asked what their procedure was for offering a new product to their buyers and gave me their email address. (No response).

OCTOBER

Thursday 5th October

My early morning visitors to the website have been missing for the past two days. I may be barking up the wrong tree, but I tend to suspect that they're in Asia somewhere. So, this morning I did a 'search' for National Holidays Worldwide and found a website with Public Holidays and clicked on yesterday's date. Lo and behold China is in the middle of a National Holiday (106) all this week. I can also check time zones online and see that China is approximately seven hours ahead. So, when the 'visitors' appear at 1a.m. it would be between 7 and 8 a.m. in China.

I'm just looking at my list of retailers and I see that M & S ask for samples to be sent and then they'll get back to the sender if interested. (I forget if I ever sent one – obviously if I did, there was no response).

Wednesday 11th October

I've now contacted John Lewis and a few other Department Stores. However, although my emails seem to increase the number of visits to the website, it's obviously not a good product for them, because there's been no response. (This is an interesting article by Anna Rigby at John Lewis published by The Guardian in 2012. It's about pitching products to big retailers (107).

Due to recent cutbacks, the British library no longer has a copy of the KOMPASS Business Directory however, they do appear to subscribe to Mintel, which is available in their London reading rooms, but better check first.

Wednesday 13th October

Yesterday, I decided to do some leafleting and dashed into town to hand some out. I found a good spot and was really pleased that almost everyone accepted one when offered. This resulted in quite a few website visits, but still no orders or inquiries.

I've just read some advice given to a company wanting to sell to a specific retail sector. The advice was that since they were already selling their product in a different country, they should provide evidence of this as proof of sales potential.

I'm now convinced that it's much too soon for me to approach buyers.

Tuesday 24th October

I noticed today that I've been getting visits from Russia. There seem to be a lot of websites in that general region referring their customers to my website, which is extremely odd. Out of interest, I clicked on one of the links to see what sort of company would be doing such a thing. It sounded like a legal firm, so I thought it would be safe enough. Not the case though, because I suddenly received a 'High Alert Intruder' warning from my Antivirus provider, who did their job and blocked it. One of the browsers being used to visit the site was Kkman, which is apparently Chinese, and the referring pages have a very wide range of names. Also, it feels as if I'm becoming addicted, because I can't stop checking the thing.

Although I sent off an 'Application to Strike-off' my redundant company name over a month ago, when I checked, the company was still on the register. So, I need to sort this out.

Wednesday 25th October

At last, I'm starting to understand site analytics and can vaguely identify where the visits are coming from. I can see that today I had 7 visits before 9 a.m. of which 5 were from Russian referring pages. I've no idea what to think.

I've now altered the T&Cs in accordance with the Commercial Manager's comments. All he wanted was for me to change the bits which related to non-delivery, because without confirmation that the goods have been received, I can't invoice the customer.

The latest brain teaser is that people seem to be visiting the 'Contact Us' page quite a lot recently. However, no emails have been arriving at the .co.uk address, which is the one I always use and is stipulated on the website. But I haven't set up a .com email address yet, which is the one connected to the website. So, I've now corrected this and have just run another test message. I shall check later to see if it's arrived at one or other of the addresses.

I still have three more pharmacies to contact. However, with nobody buying or providing feedback I have nothing to substantiate my claim that it really works yet.

Thursday 26th October

It was impossible to sleep after I woke up at 1.30 a.m. So, I got up to find out why my message hadn't arrived from the 'Contact Form'. I thought perhaps that I hadn't completed the set-up phase correctly and as it turns out I was right. So, I've now opened the additional 'set up' section and made sure that any messages will be sent to the .co.uk address. I've also activated this by clicking on 'start' or something similar. It seems that this process was vital and all this time, if people have been sending the company emails, they haven't arrived. It's maddening.

The 'site analytics' dance continues. I've now started checking even more regularly, if that's possible, and one of my recent visitors was a French Business Directory. I think these visitors must be 'spider bots' and directories are simply crawling over any unknown websites to see if they need to know about new products. There is also a visit listed from a website related to motor vehicles! The primary hits are on the 'Contact Us' page which makes me think of directories, as the address and company details are there. I'm starting to give myself a headache.

Friday 27th October

In the broad light of day, it's become apparent that I'm not getting the right kind of traffic visiting the website. It's now 11.00 a.m. and the website has 'supposedly' had 17 hits so far, 18 if you include my access in the middle of the night. The problem is, the visitors all seem to be from Russia with one from Ukraine, in which case they are not interested customers at all. One even looks as if it's a porn website. I've just looked at the referring pages for yesterday with 16 hits and they are all Russian again (or appear to be). Looking back at the last 30 days (287 visits), the story seems to be the same. Referring pages all Russian, French or Ukrainian. (Not long after this, these strange visitors went away).

I think it might be an idea to use independent selling agents. These professionals will already have access to a range of buyers, and if they're already selling to my potential customers, might be willing to add the product to their list. They can probably be found at exhibitions or on specialist websites, but the latter are likely to charge a fee. Furthermore, the use of agents means that I'd need to increase the price a little to take sales commission into account.

Monday 30th October

This morning, I realised that it was time to snail mail the radio presenter in Kent and send her a sample. My idea is to ask her to encourage listeners to get in touch for a free gadget and take part in a trial. I've mentioned that I hope to make the product available on Amazon and this seems to make good sense now. I have a little stock to sell on eBay, but if the radio host manages to garner enough interest and I end up receiving a lot of enquiries, this would provide me with sufficient evidence to take out a loan and I could then sell via Amazon as well. (No response from radio host).

NOVEMBER

Friday 10th November

I've been concerned recently, that I might not have sufficient funds in the company's PayPal account to cover the cost of the eBay seller fees, so have just checked their website. It seems that I've provided details of my bank account, so that if there are insufficient funds in the PayPal one, the money can be taken from that. What a relief. (Correction – read entry for the 5th of January).

Monday 13th November

I've been scanning the Daily Mail and Express but can't work out how to submit anything because all their articles seem to be produced by their own people. So, I've contacted a regional paper instead. I really need to work on some free publicity.

Tuesday 14th November

I've just looked up the owner of the domain name that I may want to register. Not really expecting it to be available, I went to Whois.com (108) , but it wouldn't give me the name of the owner, just the registrant. However, when I went to Nominet (109), which is the official registry for all .uk domains and then clicked on 'Who is', I could see that the name I want had been registered in 1997 to an American Corporation and is still in force. So, the other website, simply told me that the domain name was registered, but not to whom. I expect the same company owns the .com name as this seems to be the usual practice.

Tuesday 21st November

I knew I was avoiding the diary but hadn't realised that I'd left it for so long. It's been a rather disappointing week as I sent off the news release and it was rejected, with a suggestion that if I could give it a 'good news angle' such as 'I'm going to be on the radio', then it would be acceptable. I shall have to keep this in mind.

DECEMBER

Friday 1st December

I've just checked email and because I remembered to attach a 'read receipt request' there were 9 'read receipts' waiting in my inbox. I have to say though, that I rather dread going into email now just in case things suddenly take off and I need to leap about.

JANUARY

Friday 5th January

I had difficulty finding my PayPal Account number and so did others going by the number of searches made on this topic, but eventually I discovered that PayPal simply use the email address of the user (the customer). So, I went to my bank account and tried to transfer a payment of £10 to keep things ticking over for a few more months. But it wouldn't accept an email address as the reference. So, I tried something else and logged on to PayPal instead. On the left side under the Balance, there were the words 'Transfer Money'. I clicked on this and arrived at a page headed 'Transfer Money' with two blank boxes. I clicked on the top one and arrived at a page headed 'From' and a choice of either PayPal or 'My bank'. I clicked on 'My bank' and arrived back at the page headed 'Transfer money'. I could see the name of my bank in the top box so clicked on the blank box below which took me to a new page headed 'To' 'PayPal' which showed the balance in my PayPal account. I clicked on the balance and was taken back to the page headed 'Transfer money'. Now I could see from: My bank, to: PayPal and a blank box below in which to enter the amount to be transferred. So, I put in the sum that I wanted to transfer from my bank account and clicked on the confirmation button. I was then taken to a page headed 'Review' which gave the transfer details. I clicked on 'Transfer', and it was done. I think it said that the transfer would take place in approximately five working days but forgot to make a note of the exact wording at the time.

Every now and again I do a 'search' for my product which is also my company name and it's now on a couple of pages. However, most of them seem to be sites that charge a fee, offering information that is freely available on the Companies House website.

Wednesday 10th January

Not wishing to throw in the towel too easily, but not willing to spend any more money, I've decided to target Boots and Lloyds Pharmacies just on the off chance that they might be keen to see something new. So, I've written to Boots at groupprocurement@boots.co.uk. The chap who answered the phone at Head Office, said that my product information would take a few weeks to process and that they would pass my email to the buyer, if there was any interest. I'm giving them 4 weeks and will then send the same email to Lloyds Pharmacy, which is owned by Celesio a German company, part of the US multinational McKeeson Corporation. Boots is now owned by the US multinational Walgreens.

Friday 12th January

In a recent report it was indicated that a lot of retailers are starting to focus on 'own brand' products, to generate loyalty and get more shoppers through their doors.

Wednesday 24th January

There hasn't been much to write recently, except that I've decided that it's silly to wait for a response from Boots, because if they aren't interested, they simply won't respond. I'll have wasted a month or more for no good reason. So, I'm going to try and send a similar email to Lloyds Pharmacies. I could only get the buyer's name but not her email address from the Head Office switchboard, so I finally gave up on my various email combinations and let them put me through to the department. I find it very difficult to cold call buyers, so was delighted when it was answered by an assistant who gave me the information that I needed. So, my email was better this time and went to the correct buyer's email account @celesio.co.uk. (No response)

FEBRUARY

Thursday 15th February

I'm becoming rather fed up as I just keep throwing my time and money at this project for no reward. When the website was off-line yesterday, as I'd taken it down in annoyance, according to site analytics it received about 40 visits. Now I'm really confused.

Monday 19th February

I've just found some information about selling into the EU. This is along the lines that if you're a manufacturer, it's your responsibility to carry out a conformity assessment, set up the technical file, issue the EC Declaration of Conformity (110) (DoC) and place the CE marking on the product. If you're a distributor, it's your duty to check for the presence of both the CE marking and the necessary supporting documentation. It seems that I will have to be extremely vigilant if I want to export to the EU.

MARCH

Saturday 3rd March

Yesterday I was reading the online papers when I came to the bottom of an article and spotted the © mark. I then had to act quickly as I'd quoted a few lines from one or two articles on my website (and referenced it, of course). So, I took my website off-line immediately and wrote to the two papers, asking for permission to quote a couple of lines.

Friday 9th March

I suddenly received an email from one of the newspapers today, indicating that I would need to be granted a License. There would also be a charge for the use of a simple three line 'indirect' quote so far as I can understand it. Needless to say, I shan't be quoting from their website

APRIL

Thursday 19th April

I've been looking at the Gatwick Diamond (111) which is a business led organisation in the Southeast. I notice that it has a long list of sites and premises which includes business parks, and serviced offices.

Wednesday 25th April

I'm thinking that perhaps hotels and motels, which have room for a display somewhere or a vending machine, dispensing, for example, toothbrushes, shower caps and last-minute items, might be potential prospects. Most hotels are part of chains, so if I can generate some interest in this sector, then I may be able to gain 'nominated supplier' status and sell in small batches to group members. I seem to recall that hotels usually have a catalogue of items that management can access, so becoming a nominated supplier would get me onto the list. I could always ask for an introduction to their preferred wholesaler, if that's the way they wanted go.

I've just found a website for a vending company which according to them has 'last minute item' machines in some of the motel chains. Once the gadget has been fully tested and the packaging sorted out, it would make sense to talk to them. They supply travel accessories such as padlocks, travel plug adapters, baggage scales and toiletries. It seems they adapt the machines to fit the products chosen by the hotel. The Premier Inn for example has a chain of 750 hotels.

Thursday 26th April

It's only 2.00 p.m. and already I've had 38 hits on the site thanks to a promotional email that I sent out yesterday. Ideally, if the company was better off and had stock, I'd get in touch with the reporter who raised awareness of the problem my gadget solves in their original article dated 25th April. Ditto all the other commentators/reporters who've been publishing articles throughout the year. But to do so now could become a headache should I receive too many inquiries.

MAY

Monday 6th May

Editing the diary over the past couple of weeks has flagged up some opportunities that I could now investigate. Unfortunately, I still need to find money from somewhere for packaging and of course trials don't seem to be on the cards at present, which is a bit of a nuisance.

I've just come across a website which gives quite a lot of advice on using social media, Facebook, Instagram, LinkedIn and X for advertising and creating a customer base. There's also a good video about using X cards, which enable you to add more information to your tweet via a link that you can create using meta-tags etc. It seems very complicated but it's something I want to learn more about.

Monday 7th May

Today, I couldn't open my diary again which now has the Acrobat symbol beside it. In the past I could, so this is a new experience. Instead of flying into a panic when I received the pop-up message 'Adobe Acrobat Reader could not open (name of file) etc.' I thought I'd try to open it in Word. So, I've just right clicked on the document and then 'open with' then 'Microsoft Word' which seems to work.

Wednesday 9th May

I was happy today to find that when I did a 'search' for my company/gadget name, Google came up with the new introduction. This mentions that it's the real deal embracing both science and innovation, with photographs below. So, all these 'bots that I've noticed are at least doing their job.

Sunday 13th May

When I came online this morning, I decided to check whether I could clean up my files, so I had to click on 'this PC' > right click on 'local disc C:' > 'properties' > 'clean up system files'. I then clicked on 'defragment' but it said that it was on 'auto-defragment' at set intervals, so I left it.

Monday 14th May

I'm going to have one last push today to try and find a grant. There's a website on the.GOV.UK website headed 'Financial Support for Business'

(112). The website is self-explanatory and a tick-box exercise. I haven't managed to find any grants though.

For younger people between 18 and 30, I'm led to believe that the Kings Trust (113) has an excellent reputation for supporting young entrepreneurs.

I'm discovering that the UK Government provides a lot of funding to keep 'consultants' in work, but little in the way of grants for actual producers of new products, unless they relate to science and technology.

I've just received a very helpful email from Finance South-East (114). It says that I can contact the government's Business Helpline on 0300 456 3565 (at today's date) and that they offer free consultations with Business Advisers and access to a range of free business support resources. Perhaps if I give them a call, they'll point me in the right direction.

They also mention the government's Business Finance Support Finder, which is a directory of all the organisations providing government-

backed support to small businesses. This seems to be the one I've already checked and found nothing appropriate – for this business anyway.

Crowdfunding was recommended to me by one of the start-up support groups, so I've been looking at one of these websites. To be honest I think this looks very involved and requires a lot of social media use which I'm not familiar with yet.

While in edit mode, I'm just doing a bit more searching and have found a UK website which provides a list of help. However, I now realise that it's just a ploy to attract potential customers, so I won't put a link here.

I'm now looking at the Prowess (115) website which is dedicated to helping women. I've had a look around anyway and a good piece of advice on here is to get customers to pay in full up-front or at least 50% to keep the cash flowing.

I've just received a quote from an acetate box company, stating clearly 'Terms of Payment pro forma' which means up-front.

I've reached a website that's using the UK government's colours, and it appears that I might

be eligible to take part in a competition for a £1,000 grant. Reading on, I discover that the website is owned by a Media Company, so I find the colour choice very misleading. I don't think I'm very interested in competitions at this stage, perhaps once everything starts to take off.

Tuesday 29th May

I got up just now to exchange another email with my ISP. I should add that it's now 2.53 a.m. At the start of this diary, I was continuing to receive invoices for a service that I'd cancelled. Now it seems I'm back in an argument again, having just cancelled the website contract. But this is not the main problem at present.

Today the computer won't identify the memory stick, and it has my entire diary typed on it as I'm no longer trusting my laptop. This means I no longer have a digital copy and shall need to retype the lot.

I'm asking the computer for help now and 'searched' 'computer won't recognise my memory stick'. According to one forum contributor with a similar problem, they managed to open theirs on a different computer. There's now a conversation about drive letters. It looks as if I may have messed up when removing/not removing the memory stick.

Wednesday 30th May

I've just paid a visit to a computer store where they tested the memory stick. It seems that I've probably caused the problem myself, by leaving it plugged in on too many occasions, because there wasn't even a flicker of life from it. I confess that I sometimes forget to remove it, then at start-up if I realise this, have panicked and snatched it out; so, it's unlikely to be gremlins but my own ineptitude combined with a poor memory. I was told that nothing can be done and that it would cost over £100 to get the chip out and the data recovered, so this is not an option.

I've suddenly decided that I'll renew the website for another year because there could be another opportunity. Perhaps the company won't need to have a proven record of sales if I offer the gadgets on a 'sale or return' basis. It's possible the buying decision will be made by individual hotel managers rather than Head Office. (Sale or return wasn't a good idea as it turns out).

I've been offered a renewal discount of 50% by my ISP so will see if this is still available. Strangely, although I'm sure that I cancelled the direct debit details in my account, they were still there when I checked to put them back in. I'll have to be more careful in future and double check, perhaps a week or so later, that things really are cancelled.

JUNE

Tuesday 5th June

I've located a vending machine/supplies company that sells into several hotel chains and have sent them an email. So far, they haven't responded. (They never did).

I'm now doing a 'search' for wholesale gadget supplies and seem to have found something. Unfortunately, I can't work out which category my product would fit into, so will come back later. I've browsed a few more wholesale sites, but their prices are too low for me to consider them as a customer. I expect they stock-up with low-cost imports from countries with low labour costs.

Friday 8th June

Today I'm working on 'packaging on a mini budget' for my samples. To help me create my mock-up, I've used a clear acetate notelet box with euro-slot that I've purchased from a card shop.

I've just found a website which appears to supply photographs under the Creative Commons Zero (CC0) License. They appear to be free to use for any purpose with one or two caveats, which need to be checked out. It's important that I read and understand the legal explanation. I'll check on Wikipedia (116).

Saturday 9th June

I've managed to generate some blurb for my packaging and have sent it to the printer for a quote. Hopefully I'm not in the doghouse for making so many changes last time and they'll be happy to do some more work for me. My budget is very small of course, but I know the artwork will be about £30 and the cutter £50 so it's just the card and printing that I don't know about. I've asked for 50 so I can try out the new format. Fingers crossed.

Tuesday 12th June

I think I may not have sent information to Lloyds Pharmacies after all as nothing appears in my 'sent' list. It seems I may not be giving the computer sufficient time to send all the attachments before logging off. Now I must get used to watching the 'almost invisible' timeline. Perhaps I'll send another email a bit later. (This is still pending).

I've been thinking about pricing and feel sure that the product needs to cost around £12.99 to move at any pace, especially from vending machines.

Monday 18th June

I've just been reminded about the possibility of selling through an existing supplier. This would mean that a company, which already has access to a buyer and for whom an account has been set up, might be interested in adding my gadget to their existing list. If my existing supplier were to offer to be my intermediary, it would make sense for both of us, as it would increase their sales to us and give them a commission on top. (I could be repeating myself here – sorry if so).

First things first though, I want to get some product into the Premier Inn, or at least, into their vending machines. It's just a question of how quickly I can get the 3D printed samples.

Tuesday 19th June

I'm just browsing London's Excel Exhibition (117) website to see whether there are any suitable shows that I can attend this year. Sadly not. (You may find this and many other websites easier to explore on your laptop).

I paid a visit to the printer while I was in the area and was delighted to see that they've installed a new printing machine. I really like this company because they have a friendly and personal touch when it comes to dealing with their customers. I dropped off the packaging mock-up so they could see the dimensions etc. and will receive a quote by the end of the week.

Wednesday 20th June

I'm about to receive a call from the Enterprise Growth Hub but haven't prepared at all. The subject will be 'where to find a grant and where to find help with trials?'

Well, that was a helpful discussion which has really motivated me. It was actually a call from the Business Support Help Line email: enquiries@businesssupporthelpline.org Tel. 03004 563 565. It seems that some growth hubs have chat pop-ups on them run by this agency, so when I thought that I was chatting to the growth hub, it was really the government business support helpline. I received some excellent advice about where I might source some funding but there was no help with grants as these are very few and far between and aimed primarily at high tech. start-ups.

One idea put forward, not for the first time, was that I might wish to consider crowdfunding. It seems that in many cases, this doesn't involve the sale of equity, as I had thought. Furthermore, it could give the product useful publicity without going too mad. It seems some of these sites charge something like £500 for their service, but a few have a no-win no-fee structure which is the one I would obviously target if I chose to go down this route. (The address doesn't appear to work at the moment, so I typed 'get help and support for your business – GOV.UK' into the .GOV.UK search panel).

Apparently at *Start up Loans (118)* ***another fund holder that has been suggested, they are able to lend any amount up to £25K at a 6% p.a. interest rate, which has to be better than my bank.*** It says on their website that any loan is unsecured, and government backed, so no assets or guarantors are required. Loans range from £500 to £25,000. I've just checked what it would cost for an overdraft and it's horrible. I'll receive an email shortly from the advisor with all sorts of links and hub details. (I've added some comments about personal guarantees somewhere which it's important to fully understand, to avoid losing the shirt off your back. Please remember that loans must always be repaid).

Another suggestion was to get in touch with Innovate UK (*119). I've already sent them a brief email saying that I'm looking for a grant but received a negative response. The advisor said to keep knocking on their door, because that's what they're there for – to help inventors and innovators, as the name implies. (I've now noticed that they have an innovation funding link but there's nothing here for me).

I do feel that it's time to get out and talk to these support services and with any luck they might help me arrange some trials.

Quick note to self. Independent pharmacies might be willing to trial the gadget, so long as I can provide them with a counter display stand and do this on a sale or return basis. Now I'm thinking of motorway service stations.

Thursday 21st June

Rather than getting involved with enterprise agencies, which would involve a lot of phone calls and travelling, my time might be put to better use by getting the product packaged and ready for sale.

I've found a website that does counter display stands for very little money, so this could be the way to get them tested.

This morning, I emailed another acetate box company for a quote. They talk about themselves as John and Jenny which makes the firm seem flexible and friendly. They also indicate that small orders are acceptable.

Sunday 24th June

I've now received a second quotation for acetate/clear PVC boxes which is an improvement. The first gave a price of £336.00 for 500 boxes plus £125 for the cutting form; the second from John and Jenny quoted £215.00 for 500 plus £135.00 for tooling. I've 'searched' for 'cutting form' and discovered that it's the machine that folds the box into shape. So, I expect my search on these two at Companies House, will show a figure against tangible fixed assets.

The second company's name hasn't immediately come up on Companies House 'search' so I've gone back to their website and found the company number at the bottom of their home page. It should always be easy to find. Mine's under the heading Legal Notice. They've noted fixed assets worth over £200,000 at the top of their accounts, so I expect this relates in part to machinery. I must refresh my memory about depreciation at some stage, which reduces the value of some assets, and I like to know as much as possible. Asking questions online is so easy.

I've told the second company that I'm very interested, but as this is a start-up and may need to operate on a sale-or-return basis in the short term, a price for 200 units would be preferable. It's always nice to work with small companies, because they're able to make quick management decisions.

I've just received an email from the second acetate box company, and they can supply 250 rather than 500 units initially. They also have a cutting tool which I might like to take advantage of, with only slightly different dimensions which would save on cost. The quote is for £155.00 plus VAT which I can manage.

I've asked the printer, whether their artwork service might include providing a suitable photograph for the front of the packaging.

While editing, I've just checked my link to The Entrepreneur Handbook (120). There is something here called the Research and Development Tax Credit Scheme and it seems that I might be able to reclaim up to 32% of my development costs each year. This might be worth looking into. On further reading this is only for those in the science and technology sector. All the other grants are very specific but there's nothing here for this company. There do seem to be a lot though, so I'm glad I read the list. There's information on the Kings Trust (121) for example, which provides grants and loans for 18 – 30 year olds. They have all sorts of support on their website including a business plan template.

Tuesday 26th June

My search for acrylic counter display units has been quite productive. I've chosen a three-tier unit for £4.02 ex. VAT plus delivery. This will display just three items, but they can be replaced from under the counter as soon as one is sold. I've also requested samples of cello-bags from another supplier; together with some gold mailing bags to attract buyer attention and blue polythene postal bags for mail order.

I was sent just two blue postal bags, which arrived the following day and were perfect for mail order as they would pass easily through the mailing slot, but that's all.

It would be too expensive to have the product name printed onto the acetate boxes for the moment, as I've been quoted for a minimum print run of 5,000. Instead, I shall print the brand and slogan onto photographic paper and insert it into the base myself or ask my printer to do this for me.

In response to my request for a photo, my printer has sent me a link to Adobe Stock (122) which he says they use for this type of work. (You'll probably need a laptop for this website). I'm confused though as he asked me to give him the number of my choice, but I can't find any. Perhaps I need to register or something. I'm now waiting for further advice. (Fotolia is now Adobe Stock and at today's date they are offering 10 photos if you take part in a 30-day free trial).

Wednesday 27th June

I've found the following statistics for supermarket market share: Tesco 27.8%, Sainsbury's 15.8%, Asda 15.3%, Morrisons 10.4%, Aldi 7%, Co-op 6.3%, Lidl 5.2%, Waitrose 5.1%.

I'm thinking that as soon as I get into the hotel sector and sales are sufficiently buoyant, this would be the time to ask Sainsbury's if they're interested.

If I start to think about exporting, I'll be reading advice on the GOV.UK website. Starting to

Export (123) ***and*** ***Exporting and doing business Abroad (124).***

International buyers across the globe are obviously familiar with importing goods nowadays, because so much is sourced in China. Therefore, I don't imagine it would be an issue for any of them, so long as I set everything up to run smoothly. Great samples are going to be essential of course.

Overseas Sales Agents should be considered quite early on too, as the local competition will be quick to elbow their way in if I'm seen to be making a profit. One of the really important benefits of owning the patent (20 year life subject to payment of renewal fees) and registered design right (25 years ditto), is that nobody in the UK is permitted to make or sell my unique gadget other than myself or my nominated supplier. Unregistered design right (125) lasts for 10 – 15 years.

There's nothing to stop copies emerging outside the UK though due to the lack of a global patent, nevertheless 'Made in England' has always been associated with quality and is therefore a real

benefit. Perhaps 'Made and invented in England' would be even better. I'm thinking of Chinese consumers now, as customers rather than competitors. Perhaps I could start with Commonwealth Countries of which there are currently fifty-three. Even if the product doesn't prove popular here, that doesn't mean to say that it won't be appreciated in a different territory.

Saturday 30th June

Negotiating the lowest possible price from my suppliers is vital. It's possible I might be able to produce the product for under £5.00 and take advantage of quantity discounts – but buyers will expect a quantity discount themselves so it's going to be quite a juggling act.

If I try selling into the vending sector, I expect they'll be looking for a mark-up of 100% net VAT despite a very different set of overheads. Initially, with my own high purchasing costs, I could probably make a £1.00 profit on each item if I sell at a wholesale price of £6. So, my mark-up % would be balance £1.00 / cost price £5.00 x 100 = 20% or (SP £6.00 – CP £5.00 = £1.00 balance /

CP £5.00 = 20 x 100 = 20 %.) And my GP margin would be (£1.00 / £6.00 = 0.167 x 100 = 16.7%.

So, if I set the RRP at £12.99 and remove the VAT element (£12.99 x 20/120 = £2.17) = £10.82 then remove my SP £6.00 = £4.82 (the balance); their mark-up % would be £4.82 / CP £6.00 = 0.80 x 100 = 80%. As they could be looking for a 100% mark-up, I should be prepared to haggle a bit, but because they don't have the same overheads as other retailers, they may be satisfied with this. Their GP margin would be £4.82 / £10.82 = 45%.

I read somewhere, although it has escaped me now, that it's not unusual for wholesalers to sell their goods with a mark-up of around 20% but this needs further investigation and obviously depends on quantity. For my purposes I would want to achieve a 33% mark-up. Therefore, I should simply multiply my cost price £5.00 by 1.33 (33%) to find out what my selling price to the retailer should be. So, 5.00 x 1.33 = £6.65. So, I would need to set my wholesale price to the retailer at £6.65; but that would create an RRP at the point of sale to the consumer of £6.65 x 2 (100%) = £13.30 plus 20% VAT £2.66 = £15.96, a level that's likely to put a lot of customers off. I can see that I must get the goods put together for less than £5.00 if I want to sell them for £6.00. So, I'll see what a cost price of £4.50 looks like; £4.50 x 1.33 = £5.99. So, if I can reduce my variable costs to £4.50, I shall be in a much happier position.

There's also a very useful website *calculator (126)* ***which is called Omnicalculator which works out the GP Margin% and GP Mark-up %.*** (Once again you will need something more powerful than a Kindle e-reader).

The following website belonging to *Booths Supermarket (127)* ***a company in Lancashire explains step by step about how to sell to them, set your RRP and wholesale price etc.***

To undertake a little research on industry sectors and share prices, why not check-out *London Southeast (128).*

JULY

Monday 2nd July

Getting down to the fine detail now, I'm wondering how to improve my chances of attracting customers. Word of mouth is the most effective tool I think, but if the message isn't a good one, then it will be hugely problematic.

This morning, I made up my mind that I shall purchase 100 printed inserts and just buy off the shelf acetate boxes from the card shop, for the limited number of samples I shall be sending out or showing to buyers. They cost £2.50 each, but if I only buy 10 for £25.00 then it's better than spending £300 before I get any orders.

Surprisingly, I managed to find the numbered photographs at Adobe Stock quite easily today.

Tuesday 3rd July

I've been wondering how the barcode gets onto the product, so I'll have a little 'search'. It seems that the code numbers come from GS1UK (129). This is a not-for-profit organisation, and the UK membership fee is £119 per annum ex. VAT. This comes with 1,000 barcode numbers which cost extra, except for the first three. I shall probably need five called GTIN-13s if I'm to offer customers a colour choice. I'll also need the same number of code numbers called GTIN-14s for the outer cases/cartons. Bulk number purchase is available at a cost of £14 each per batch of five, £11 each per batch of 10 units etc.

The barcode image is produced in a format called EPS (Encapsulated PostScript) which is something to do with Adobe Illustrator, I think. My local GS1 office is in London. The link for the important 'Terms and Conditions' is located at the extreme bottom of each web page, which I must read when I get some free time.

Thinking again about my RRP. If I can get into the vending machine sector, rather than let the retail outlet put some random sticky price label on my beautiful packaging, I'm going to buy some removable sticky labels online and will put them on myself. I've just found some with the price of £12.99 on the top half and the Union Jack on the bottom half, so I've ordered some.

I signed up for email reminders from HMRC to let me know when my VAT return is due. As it's now arrived, I'm going to do that right away. I've nothing to pay or reclaim this quarter, but it needs to be done anyway.

Thursday 12th July

My document print quality has been getting worse over the course of time and 'deep cleaning' isn't having any effect. When I carry out 'nozzle check' I can see lots of blanks where the ink isn't getting through the print head. So, I've just been on YouTube to try and find out what could be happening. Because I use an ink refill pack which includes cleaning fluid, I've taken out the cartridge, and the print head on the base is now standing in a small plastic container to soak for a while. I've made sure that I don't touch the copper-coloured electronic circuit strip or let it get wet. If this doesn't do the trick, I'll just have to repeat the process or buy another cartridge. There are lots of videos on YouTube, but some recommendations look rather dodgy.

Today I've received the artwork from the printer, and it looks excellent. So, I've asked for the order to be placed for the cutter, which will make a smaller euro-slot than last time to match the off-the-shelf acetate boxes that I'm using. Naturally I've checked the size on hangers in some of my local chain stores and it appears to be the standard measurement. If I'd done this last time, I could have saved myself about £50.00.

Friday 13th July

Today I had to buy another cartridge as nothing I was doing seemed to make the print any clearer. The first shop was charging £27.99, so I went to another close by and bought the same one for £15.99.

Monday 16th July

On the barcode question, I think I should get this printed onto the packaging insert now, not later, as it would look much more professional and save any hassle for myself and more importantly the customer. If it's not there, then I presume the retailer would have to allocate one to it themselves and stick a barcode label on it. They might even obscure some important sales blurb on the back.

I've just received an email from my anti-virus provider, saying that the account has been auto debited for the deluxe version or something similar and thanking me. Well, that's a mistake because I know what's going on and I haven't even received the count-down warning that virus protection "will expire in 'so many' days". I forwarded the email to my associate who manages the account, accompanied by various urgent text messages. He's now checked, and the information seems to be accurate. The money has been taken. I realise now that when I clicked on Norton earlier, I didn't understand that I was asking for an upgrade to Norton's deluxe product. It was much too easily done! (Following a phone call a refund was made without any argument).

Thursday 19th July

I'm now on the GS1UK barcode website (130) and have found some information about why it is important to have your own barcode. I can see, as I suspected, that the first 9 digits will be the numbers which will identify the company. The other digits are used to identify the product/s. The number also indicates the company location and there's a check number in there for safety. The correct name for a barcode is a Global Trade Item Number (GTIN).

It seems that once I'm registered, GS1UK enables me as the GTIN licensee, to create my own GTIN-13 barcodes (131) via their website and the image can be checked for readability by them too (validation). However, if as with my product it will be covered by light reflecting plastic packaging, the whole pack will probably need to be sent to one of their recommended partners for them to check (verification).

Friday 20th July

It seems that I can produce my free GTIN-13 code numbers by clicking on 'create'. After downloading these to my computer I can email them as attachments to my printer. He will then open them with dedicated software and print the barcodes onto the inserts. One extra GTIN-13 will cost £16.00.

However, it seems that only the GTIN-14 'code number' for the outer case/carton can be generated by GS1 from the GTIN-13 (at no extra

cost) but not the image file, so I shall need to use one of their partners, or some dedicated software to turn it into the actual barcode image. Apart from this, the only difference seems to be that the GTIN-14 starts with the number one, and the last digit/digits are different, but I could be wrong. I'm told that there should be some free barcode imaging software available to download online if I want to go down that path.

Once the cost of the GTIN-14 'creation' has been added to the GS1 price of £16.00 – one quote I received was £15 - it will have cost me about £31 in total. The GTIN-14 will then be ready for me to send to my printer unless I choose to use the GS1UK partner to print the outer case/carton labels.

I've accidentally deleted my whole document – thank heavens I knew to click on the back-arrow at the top left of the toolbar. I have no idea how I did that.

Saturday 21st July

Now I'm looking on Wikipedia for GS1, but before long I've found myself on GS1US.org (132) the US website.

All these searches may take time, but it's helped me to understand that doing things correctly from the outset is very important. I can now see that traceability is a hugely important benefit, not just for me, but also for my customers. I've decided that my very own company GTIN sometimes called a European Article Number (EAN) is a vital piece of (licensed) intellectual property and like the patent, it will need to be renewed each year to sell efficiently on a global basis. I want one of these.

There used to be a video on the GS1UK site explaining the benefits of using barcodes but on checking it's not where it was, so I'd recommend reading the FAQ's page..

Monday 23rd July

I noticed yesterday, when I was getting my cash book up to date, that my bank has increased their fee for an unauthorised overdraft, from 2.2% as a first-year start-up, to 26.4%. So, no bank charges for the first 18 months, but increases in other fees after one year. But you'll obviously need to check with your own bank as these figures will vary.

Monday 30th July

Today I'm back to learn more about barcodes. I've noted that many retailers require a barcode verification report from a 'GS1 partner', to prove that the barcode will scan quickly and accurately every time. This 'verification' (not validation) check, which I mentioned above, is more rigorous than validation and is carried out on the final packaging, which could be light reflective, just for example and might need modifications.

I'm assuming that if or when hotels place their first order I'll be directed towards their 'supplier' web page and will discover what type of barcode they expect me to use on the 'outer cases' if any. This will include the quantity, colour and any other essential information that they need. This could be a GTIN-13, GTIN-14 which can also be called an ITF-14, a GS1-128 or a Code 39. There's also a more recent barcode design known as a GS1 Data Matrix. This is a 2D barcode consisting of black and white cells in a square or rectangular pattern, which carries even more information, or a QR Code which can be read by a smartphone with the appropriate software.

I think I need a break from all this barcode stuff so I'm going to reflect on another story that was once shared with me. There were once two friends. One invented and the other did not. The one who did not, expressed an interest in investing as part of a group in his inventor friend's great idea for which he had just been granted a patent. I think it was £50,000 for 25%. Then suddenly at the very last minute, the friend revealed that one of their group had consulted their accountant and the offer had been changed to 51% of equity with a buy-back option. It sounds as if the inventor wasn't too pleased. Everything had been agreed except on paper and now his so-called friend and his co-investors were trying to take control of his company. Understandably, he told his 'friend' to get lost. But I think they were right to consult an accountant, and he might have tried negotiating instead of losing his temper. However, looking at the scenario as an outsider, I suspect the accountant could have had his eye on the work which he would surely have been given had the inventor lost control. Also, one of the investors hoped to be given a key role, which the inventor didn't feel they'd be suited to and later felt that this was probably key to their group decision-making process. I don't think you could blame them really. It was a lot of money to part with and no guarantee of success. If he had parted with 51% though, he would have had no option but to accept all their joint decisions. Just because somebody has money, they should not be able to buy themselves a key job that they're unsuited to, is what he thought. With the benefit of hindsight, he suspected that their plan was to remove him as Managing Director and take control of the company.

AUGUST

Wednesday 1st August

I've just learned that if a website is secure the prefix to the address is https: whereas if it is not secure the prefix is http: I must remember this and there should always be a padlock symbol before the address or clearly displayed elsewhere in the browser window, before I provide any financial or other confidential information. So 'look for the 'S' and the padlock', will be my mantra from now on. (I later read somewhere that it's not difficult to obtain the padlock and it can be placed on dodgy websites, so always be careful). Interesting read here on the BBC website.

Apparently I can help my website to be found more easily online by using GS1 Smart Search (133). However, I've read what's on this link and it seems that I would need a technician to set it up. It seems to be akin to search engine optimization (SEO).

Reflecting on all the above, membership of GS1UK seems to be an excellent idea as it

enables the licensee to upload their product information onto a central database. This links the product to the legitimate brand owner and their location by global location number (GLN), which is part of the GS1 barcode.

Thursday 2nd August

I've been thinking about my marketing strategy, which must be rather minimalist as there's no budget. As soon as I receive the inserts, I'll visit some hotels and talk to receptionists to get their feedback. Once I'm confident enough in my presentation, I'll telephone the ones where I received the best response and make an appointment to meet with the appropriate manager. I'll choose hotels where the desk isn't busy, and the receptionist has time to chat. I'll also be able to gauge whether it would work in a counter display. (I was useless at this).

I've just realized that when I visited Adobe Stock earlier to find a photograph for the packaging, I needed to click on the image that I was interested in, to see the photo number.

I've been looking at images of vending machines in 'search' and so long as the retaining bar at the front is of the swirl type, it will be possible for customers to read the product name at the bottom of the pack. I can see that in the picture I'm looking at, the size of the product holder is adjustable. I've just clicked on another image for a machine dispensing toiletries (134) which the owner claims was taken in a Premier Inn. (Left click on image to enlarge). One of the products is a selfie stick priced at £15.00, so my gadget would fit into their price range. Putting on a £12.99 price sticker would obviously not work for vending, as their pricing is in whole numbers such as £3.00 or £3.50. On looking more closely, it states that 1p and 2p coins are not accepted anyway, which means that 99p just doesn't work. The packs are not priced – it is just on the machine. I've put the link above in case I need another look.

I've just looked for my company on the Companies House website to check when the accounts are due. It seems that they need to be there by the 23rd of August. The Confirmation Statement is due on the 22nd of November and at the very latest must be filed by the 6th of December.

Friday 3rd August

I decided to defragment disc space first thing today as I seem to have lost more memory. It's very random. This morning, I had 900+MB but now that I've run the defrag tool in System C: > Properties, I only have 694MB. So, I've 'searched' 'defragmentation just lost my space' and it seems there are lots of people with the same problem.

Sunday 5th August

Yesterday afternoon, I spent quite a lot of time looking through my document files and deleted any that I thought I could do without. What I've discovered though, is that when I've been scanning a single document and saving it to 'documents' the scanner has saved a whole string of photographs via something called 'my document garden'. Everything has been made far too complicated, and I know I've sent a lot of photos to somebody in error which is very annoying.

Monday 6th August

I'm looking at the list of 'services' offered by GS1UK 'partners' which is located to the right of their screen. I want to learn more about 'Advanced Shipping Notifications' (ASNs) but suspect that this will be part of any electronic document interchange (EDI) system, which my logistics provider will have. I've just checked with 'search' and am looking at the answers to questions already being asked. EDI is simply the exchange of documents between trading partners. I imagine one example could be those transactions between Amazon and their customers.

I've been thinking about selling to a wholesale intermediary in the cash and carry sector, but if I don't raise the RRP to let them take a slice of the profits, the company will go out of business. The RRP is a crucial factor when it comes to attracting customers, so this is a serious issue. I'm starting to see why China has become a key player in keeping prices down, but at a high cost to UK manufacturing jobs and to my mind, quality. This is why I'm going to read everything I can find on YouTube about Supply Chain Management.

Well, it didn't take long because it was all stuff that was mostly common sense. But I do need to make plans as to how to manage stock as the company expands. Buyers will not have the confidence to place an order unless they can be assured of a quick response to their needs. Delivery needs to be within seven days and my main supplier has quoted 6 – 8 weeks. This means I need to carry stock. Thank goodness the product is small!

I'm looking at DHL (135) who offer a warehousing and fulfilment service - a bit like Amazon but without the sales angle - and have contacted them to ask for some prices. (There seems to be nothing suitable).

I've just typed 'Webinars' into the search box on the GS1UK website. There's something here about eBay changes so I must read this. It seems that eBay are producing a new product catalogue with GTINs at their core. They now want sellers to input their GTIN numbers, which I don't really understand since I always thought this site was primarily aimed at those who want to trade in second-hand merchandise. They keep using the acronym PBSE. Having looked this up, it stands for 'People Buy and Sell Everyday'.

Wednesday 8th August

This morning, I emailed my printer asking him to send me the insert proof with barcode, so that I can get it validated (not verified) by GS1UK. This needs to be done before printing takes place, just in case they have any recommendations to make. If one of the partners print the carton labels, I wouldn't expect to need this validation. (The way I remember the difference between validation and verification is to recall that my friend Val always comes first)

Sunday 12th August

Overnight I seem to be losing more memory. I've just 'searched' to check the lifespan of a desktop computer, and it seems to be about 4 – 5 years; so, I'm going to back everything up on memory sticks ready for the inevitable. I've read that the capacitors on the mother board only have an average lifespan of 5 years; RAM (random access memory) or perhaps I mean ROM (read-only memory) too, and that it physically degrades. It was because I suddenly remembered that most things are set to fail after a certain period, that I even thought to 'search' the question of lifespan. It seems my time's up, and I'll need to juggle cash flow once again.

I need to renew the gadget patent this month, so that's another £110 that I must find from somewhere.

On Monday I'll visit some small independent hotels with free samples including the display stand. This will at least provide me with the trial that I need and some publicity. I'm now going to look on YouTube and try to learn some selling skills. (This might have helped, but I'm ashamed to say that I never looked).

Sunday 19th August

I've just discovered that I need to be in 'edit' mode to be able to close the 'header' function. In the past, like many others, I've had to look online to see how to get out of this. Eventually I discovered that clicking on 'escape' (Esc) would do the trick, but I'm glad I've found the correct method.

I'm seriously considering putting the product on Amazon as well as eBay as soon as I have some stock.

I may already have typed this note, but I was having difficulty yesterday uploading a photograph of the new packaging onto my website, until I suddenly realized that the camera wouldn't talk to the computer until I had selected PC. I also learned that I need to open the photograph in 'Paint', to save it in a format that the website would accept, which I could achieve by clicking on 'save as' and then JPEG. (More recently I learned that if my photo is too small, I can enlarge it in 'Paint' prior to saving it in JPEG etc.).

The new packaging looks good now and should attract a bit of attention at the check-out desk.

Monday 20th August

Up early to 'search' for overdraft fees. I had a feeling that they were going to be a lot higher than I expected. So, I've searched, and they do seem to be very high. For example, it appears that they are calculated daily and if I were to take out an overdraft of £1,500 which is what I really need to get going and use it all, it would cost me 1,500/7 = 215; 215 x 1p. = £2.15 per day. Which means x 30 = £64 per month. The calculation is that I would pay £0.01p for every £7.00 that I borrow.

Another bit of excitement this morning. I came to read the online papers, and suddenly a whole load of horizontal barcode looking images started to flash all over the screen accompanied by a continuous buzzing sound, so I hastily switched off. Restarting just gave me a blank screen, but when I tried again after a few minutes, everything seemed to be back, except that my documents were all missing once more. Memory is now down to 104MB which probably accounts for this.

Tuesday 21st August

Having recently placed an order for 50 units with my supplier, this morning I discovered an email from her advising that the price has been increased by 30 pence per unit! If this is going to happen every year without warning, how can an accurate RRP ever be set? My customers will expect a quantity discount, but I've just lost a chunk of my profits. Perhaps high street retail is the wrong path. I'll now need to start looking for an alternative supplier as a matter of urgency. If they can make the part for less, I'll switch and keep the unreliable one as a back-up.

Friday 31st August

Well, as I was saying, the computer's been totally misbehaving with flashing images etc. and finally gave up the ghost completely. So now I'm typing on a borrowed laptop.

This wasn't the end of my problems though, because the printer didn't seem to be working – then a friend mentioned that I probably needed to download the drivers, so I've just finished doing that.

An initial concern was that whenever the screen was awake but inactive, it suddenly went black and a wavy purple message, rather like a screen saver appeared saying 'HI GET OUT NOW'. So, this had me really worried thinking it was a virus! I then typed 'screensaver' into the programs 'search' box and discovered that this was indeed a 'screensaver', so I've changed it to bubbles. Now to get on with some work.

On Wednesday I received my order for 25 units. (I reduced the order by 50% when I was informed about the price increase).

At lunch time today, I took all my samples and visited three random hotels. The first was more of a B & B and had no front desk, the second only had a part-time receptionist who would be called to perform other duties at the drop of a hat and thought the gadgets might be stolen in her absence.

The third, however, was a much larger hotel and I believe independent. There was a full-time receptionist at the desk, but the manager was on leave until the 14th. When I tried to explain what the product was, I was hopeless, because it really needs a demonstration. But I did manage to leave a sample.

It seems however, that my original plan to target smaller hotels is a nogoer, due to reception arrangements, but at least I now know this. In the past I've made appointments to meet the manager so shall now resort to this strategy. (I didn't of course as the plans changed)

SEPTEMBER

Sunday 2nd September

Somewhat energized by yesterday's trip and aware that there are four hotels with permanently manned receptions in the area, I've now visited The Hilton, Premier Inn, Travelodge and one other hotel with my more professionally prepared samples.

The Hilton reception was very polished and clutter free (hopefully they have a vending machine). Premier Inn also, but I think it might work at the counter. The next one which shall remain nameless wasn't very friendly and was in a noisy area, with a bar and everybody eating breakfast close by. However, best of all was the Travelodge and I was able to speak to the Manager who was in reception.

The first two gave me the name of the Manager so that I could call later, but the nameless one refused, insisting that the manager would contact me if he/she was interested. Nevertheless, I believe that sample distribution is the best idea yet because there are now 15 of my beautifully packaged gadgets in circulation. (I did call one of these and was asked to email, which I did, but there was no response).

Thinking about how both manufacturers have just put up their prices by 10p and 30p, I think that when I'm asked for a discount by the buyer, I'll say that I need to talk to my suppliers and get back to them. I must do so much work to get this product out, whereas they only need to do more of the same.

Tuesday 4th September

I'm just checking the company accounts of a firm that I'm interested in working with and have searched the terms 'fixed assets' and 'intangible assets' to refresh my memory.

I've decided that I'm now able to purchase some packaging from my chosen acetate box supplier. My intention is to set up an Amazon account and ask a friend for some help with 'Instagram' and other social media platforms.

I'm currently filing all my emails in the correct order and have just found one from eBay. It seems that because the fee was only £0.75p and the item didn't sell, they're not billing me. I was only re-listing one item with a few alterations, but during the process I saw that a fee of £3.00 had appeared in the total. I quickly scrolled up to find that there was a box ticked by accident/automatically for something or other, which I didn't want.

I've been trying to read an invoice that I've been sent, but it won't open correctly. Suddenly I realized that this laptop may not have Adobe Acrobat Reader so I'm about to download it for free. That was easy. I can now open my invoices and any other pdf formatted documents.

Wednesday 5th September

This evening, I thought I'd start reading up on Amazon again and found a link which explains their fees well. Amazon has a much wider reach than any e-Commerce website that I might set up for the company, which would cost me something like £20 per month on a 'yearly contract'.

From what I can gather, with Amazon I can stop selling any time I want to if I sign up for an

Individual Seller account, which is an enormous plus.

Thursday 6th September

Life online is still full of surprises. Yesterday when I searched for my product, Norton Safe Search had a grey question mark against the results deterring people from clicking on the links. So, this is not good.

I managed to find a page on the Symantec (136) website and clicked on 'support' at the top of the page. (Laptop or device other than Kindle Reader probably required). Then I scrolled down and clicked on 'Contact Support' (with the headset picture) at the bottom. This took me through to LIVE CHAT which was marvellous. So, I had my chat and was sent a link by email. However, I found the information too difficult to follow, so came back again today and typed in my case number so that I could request more information. When I explained the difficulty, I was told that the senior team would sort out the problem and call me in a few days to confirm. So, if that happens and I get a 'white tick on a green sphere' all will be well.

It certainly pays to keep checking for visibility. But one positive is that when the full name is searched, my new photograph of the product in its branding, appears beside the search saying that it's available on eBay. (I've just typed in the full product title and find that I now have a large box at the top of the 'search result' page with photos and a further five links listed).

Now that I have a laptop with 360GB of space, (I needed to get a new hard drive installed) I've been able to copy the diary from the memory stick and place it in 'Documents' where I can continue to work on it.

I've just been into my eBay account and have added £1.50 postage and packing to the price which I think is reasonable. It was going to be free to attract customers, but there seems no point as everyone will know the RRP is £12.99 inclusive of VAT and expect to pay a little for postage anyway.

I've now typed into 'search' 'Sign up to Amazon as an Individual Seller' and found a link with the title: 'Sell on Amazon – Basic Selling Program – Amazon.co.uk' which links to here (137) .

Before I forget, I had a call from a Norton Antivirus engineer earlier today about the 'safe search' issue. However, when he asked to take over my computer so he could sort out the issue remotely, I said that I never allowed anyone remote access, which he was fine with.

It took a while to explain the problem, but eventually he sent me a link to a form that I could complete and ask for the engineers to investigate the issue. Currently, the website is showing as 'unsafe' if people simply type in the product name. He said it would take about 8 days to be corrected. That's fine. I just hope hotel managers haven't come across this issue and decided to give the company a wide birth.

Norton has been very good. I've just checked spam for no reason at all and found an email from Norton. They say that they've fixed the problem. Yes, they have! And it only took an hour or so. Great service – happy customer here. The product name now looks excellent on 'search' and very safe! (Re. Norton Safe Search, if I click on 'Norton Browser Extension' on the Symantec website, I can choose to submit a website to Norton Safe Search and follow the instructions).

Friday 8th September

My quick 'search' about 0844 numbers, came up with the following: 0870, 0844 and 0845 all allow for revenue to be shared between the phone service provider and the company which owns the number. These 'national' numbers appear to be popular with call centres.

A new problem now as two of my suppliers want me to pay on receipt of their pro-forma invoice (i.e. pay up front).

Tuesday 11th September

I want to broaden my supplier base, but I seem to have another problem now. According to my online research, there aren't many acetate box manufacturers left to choose from. Presumably this is because everyone has been buying their acetate boxes and other products from China. This could be advantageous to the survivors but doesn't leave UK innovators with much choice.

I've just looked in email and see that I've received a very polite letter from one of the firms

that I've been in touch with. Apparently, their search on Experian, one of the credit reference agencies, has shown my company to be 'high risk' with an advisory credit limit of £500. Well, I'm not in the least surprised because I know there won't be any information on the company yet. So, I responded to this and have been offered 30 days credit with a £500 limit following payment of their first pro-forma invoice. So, it pays to ask for credit and explain a little about the trading situation.

Wednesday 12th September

On waking up today, I decided that I should look around for an alternative supplier for one of the essential parts and was surprised to find one company that had an extremely comprehensive and professional looking website. Yet when I looked them up on the Companies House website, I discovered that they'd only started trading (or possibly been registered) a few years ago and had received 2 compulsory strike-off notices from Companies House. At least, this is how it appeared to me, so I'll keep looking.

Another firm that I've just looked up, says on their 'About Us' page that they've been established since 1995. Yet their Companies House records say incorporated in 2002, so I guess they were previously unregistered.

I've now found two that I like the look of and have sent off a quote request. One of them looks very well established, so I'll give them preference if they can give me a decent price.

Friday 14th September

I bought three more packs of cards today for the clear packaging and have prepared another sample to send to the Box Co.

Today I received a call from the commercial finance chap. I've just been checking that the factoring facility is still available whenever I'm ready. It seems that the previous manager has moved on – as they do – and I've had to send copy emails to the new one so that I don't need to repeat the whole process.

He explained how vending machine companies operate, which I thought might be a potential sales route. Apparently, they remunerate hotels for allowing them to place their machines on the premises and pay them a commission/percentage on each item sold. It seems I would have to agree to supply a certain amount of stock as required and that they would then advise me how much stock had been sold. Only at this point would I be able to submit my invoice. This is not going to help my cash-flow at all. I therefore need to concentrate on firms that I can invoice on confirmation of delivery. I've a feeling he'll want to see the updated business plan, so I'll need to get on with it.

I've decided to order 250 acetate boxes and use my existing stock to send out samples to all and sundry. One of the reasons for this is to take advantage of the smaller sum required to make a first purchase because I'll then have the 30 days credit for larger orders.

Monday 17th September

Just about any term or condition can be 'searched' it seems and one accounting term that had me flummoxed was "Directors advances, credits and guarantees". Initially I thought this meant that the Director had lent the company money, but I now understand that it is the other way around.

I've been watching an Instagram tutorial (138) on my laptop to find out how it all works. This is because my Kindle reader is not set up for YouTube.

Tuesday 18th September

Is it worth it? Is what I've been asking myself today. It's now two years since I started the company and began writing this diary. I was going to buy some acetate boxes, but that could be another £250 down the drain, so I must wonder whether it makes sense to continue.

My main supplier has put up their prices without warning by a whopping thirty pence and raising my RRP would reduce the product's sales potential. This increase is going to have a crippling effect on my profit margin which is already too low. The few manufacturers who've survived the recession, now have an opportunity to raise their prices, and there's absolutely nothing to stop my suppliers from increasing their prices again next year.

I keep thinking 'thank goodness I haven't committed to any orders yet'. The main objective of all buyers is to choose the right goods at the lowest possible price, while a lack of competition enables my suppliers to push their prices up.

All this effort for what? Something must give. I have annual payments to make for keeping the patent in force and the barcodes ditto; the website is on an annual contract paid monthly, ditto two domain contracts and the bank will be charging for services and transactions from next month.

But I do have a choice. To go on, or not to go on? That is the question. And this is solely down to the fact that I haven't borrowed one penny from the bank or anyone else!! I'm still free and perhaps more surprising – still here!!

The new knowledge that vending machine companies only accept invoices after the goods have been sold is a huge blow, messing up my factoring strategy. This was supposed to be my way of proving consumer demand which has just gone down the drain.

I've given away five counter displays full of my new gadgets to hotels and sent a follow-up letter of introduction to all but haven't received a single response! I've even sent a sample to the vending machine company and they're ignoring me.

I literally can't be bothered now to make follow-up phone calls. They say people buy from people, so I should probably be trying to make appointments for face-to-face meetings, but I'm all washed out. This is probably where I should be looking for a partner as I don't have the full skill set for this job.

Saturday 22nd September

Well, I think I've found the solution and can get around the threat of being locked into my RRP by the buyers. The risk of another price rise is too great to ignore, so I can counter this by putting up my prices as well, but only by what I'm compelled to pay my suppliers and will keep looking for alternatives. I've absolutely decided to sell direct to consumers now. Eventually another company will pop-up and create some competition for my sole supplier, especially if the country gains a greater focus on manufacturing. I'm talking about getting involved in social media and selling only on Amazon, eBay and my own e-commerce website, where I shall have absolute control over my pricing and the number of units I'm willing to sell.

I've now set up online banking for my personal current account, so that I can pay cash into the business electronically until I start making sales. It seems to be a rational way of avoiding bank fees, which from now on will be £1.00 per £100 deposited over the counter or via the deposit machine. In this way I'm hoping to avoid all charges except the monthly account fee, which comes into force next month when the 18 months free banking period expires.

Tuesday 25th September

It's quite unbelievable how a single supplier can wield so much power over my life. I wonder how many start-ups have collapsed due to such a scenario.

I've done a search on unfair price increases and came up with a report by Deloitte, but it's now disappeared. As a result, I've written to my supplier and made some suggestions. Probably not a good move but I needed to express my frustration. The article discussed the pros and cons of raising prices. It recommends giving prior notice of any price increase which makes very good sense. I was given none.

Wednesday 26th September

I haven't received a response from my supplier yet but I'm 99% sure that if I get one it will be very negative. So, I need to reflect on where I went wrong. The initial price was good enough for me to be able to work with it, and I was even offered a 5% quantity discount. The price has gone up without warning which means that the quantity discount stood for nothing, nor did the original price offer.

I went wrong, when I mistakenly believed that the quote would remain in force indefinitely and that I could even get it lowered with a quantity discount which won't come into play until the product is well established. As for selling to pharmacies and hotel chains, I'm so glad I didn't go down that route because it could have been a total disaster.

I should have heeded something that I already knew but unfortunately chose to ignore because of the perceived difficulties involved. I absolutely should have made sure that there were more manufacturers in the market, able to sell the same product part at a similar price before I started all this.

Thursday 27th September

Now I really do need to watch 'How to use Instagram for your Business' and then I want to start following some tweets on X. I shan't use the business ID for the moment as I don't want people looking at the website until I'm ready. I also need to learn how to put something on Amazon, which is probably very similar to eBay. Then there's Facebook to learn about and how it can be used for business. I also want to learn about Pinterest and Snapchat.

In the Instagram video, the woman's talking about Instagram feed and Instagram stories and the need to thank people who've commented on your posting or click on the heart, preferably visiting their account in return. Posting once a day is recommended and it's possible to see when followers are online. Apparently, it's easier to 'like' a photo than a video, I'm not sure why though. It's also recommended that the user opens two or three accounts to cover different interests.

Friday 28th September

I've been watching the American equivalent of Dragons Den on Netflix called Shark Tank. It's impossible to ignore the fact that most of the entrepreneurs appear to have been selling loads of their product on Amazon. However, they also seem to have invested enormous sums in online advertising.

I've a lot to do today such as updating the accounts and preparing for the VAT return.

I'm clicking on a list of questions that people have asked about Instagram and can see the abbreviation CPM which I've just 'searched'. It stands for 'cost per mille (thousand)' so the advertiser pays per 1,000 clicks on their advert. More on Wikipedia.

OCTOBER

Tuesday 2nd October

I've just received a very nice email from the pack and dispatch firm asking how I'm getting on. I've explained that I'm presently stuck but will get back to them if anything changes. It now seems unlikely that I'll be needing them in the foreseeable future unless I become bombarded with orders on Amazon.

Friday 5th October

Yesterday evening, I became so frustrated by the lack of response from the two manufacturers that I'd recently discovered online, that I decided to try and wake one up a bit. So, although I've no intention of paying them a visit, I emailed one to say that I'd be in their area next Wednesday (which I won't be) and would try to drop by to discuss the part that I need. This could get a response, as nobody really wants potential customers to 'drop by'. All they needed to do was let me know that they couldn't take on any more work at present and I would have been satisfied.

If they don't reply, I'll give them a call to see whether they really exist and say that my trip's been cancelled.

So, as long as I don't take on any debt; fail to complete my Corporation Tax Return or advise HMRC that no tax is due; keep filing the Annual Accounts and Annual Return (Confirmation Statement) at Companies House, I'm still in the game!

I had another go at logging in to online banking today but still can't get in, so it's back to the bank tomorrow. What a waste of time.

Tuesday 9th October

I've just put in the company bank account details again so that HMRC can either take the VAT that I owe them, or give me a rebate, which is due in this case as I haven't sold anything yet. As it's about a week since the return was due, I had to 'search' to find out the deadline, which I now know is one month and seven days after the due date.

The reason I checked, is because it says on the HMRC website (VAT section) that it'll take a

couple of days to set up the direct debit again, so until then I shouldn't try to make my VAT return. (This is because they removed my bank account details, as no repayment/payments were recorded for the last two quarters).

I've given up trying to set up an online account with the other bank and have now set it up with the same bank that I use for both my Personal and Business Account. Now I just need to wait for my authentication code to come through and I'll be ready to go. At last, I'll be able to transfer money from my personal account to the Business Account without having to pay bank charges.

Wednesday 10th October

Interestingly, the manufacturing company was uncontactable today which is when I was 'supposed' to visit. I phoned at about 9.30 and again 11.30 and each time I was diverted to a 'fax machine'. There really is something odd about this company so I need to give them a wide birth.

Friday 12th October

As I suspected, there's been a lot of activity on the website with yesterday's visits amounting to

28, four of which were search engine robots/crawlers being 'Google PageSpeed Insights', 'Googlebot', Googlebot-Mobile and bingbot/2.0. At 7p.m. and 8p.m. there were eight and twelve visits respectively. The only action I've taken that could possibly have caused this surge of interest, was to leave samples at various chemists. I guess I haven't got a clue really as I don't subscribe to the more advanced site analytics.

My Accountant's just informed me that he's retiring to Spain soon so can no longer act as the company's registered office. I've therefore moved it to a business hub which is cheaper. I've also filed form AD01 Change of Registered Office Address with Companies House.

Wednesday 17th October

My ISP has just emailed to say that my .com domain is due for renewal at a cost of £31.44 so I've paid the bill (2 years' worth). The .co.uk also comes up for renewal soon.

Thursday 18th October

I've been watching a lot more episodes of 'Shark Tank' on Netflix and many of the entrepreneurs seem to be raising money on a platform called Kickstarter. So that's what I'm reading about now. It's taken me a while to find the projects that want funding; the primary concentration seems to be on music, art, craft, dance, design, theatre etc. although there is a section on gadgets.

I'm not sure that my gadget would fit in. I nearly logged out before I saw the faintly printed word 'Discover' top left and I'm now browsing more than 2,000 projects – well the first few at least. People really need to know what they're looking for.

Friday 19th October

I've just spotted my note about VAT. I came out of the HMRC website the other day without printing off a copy of the return by mistake. Possibly, because it hadn't been accepted yet, I was unable to find it under 'view submitted returns' when I logged back in. Anyway, it's there now so I've printed a copy. It says that repayment of VAT can take up to 30 days, so not to contact them until after 21 days from the date of submission.

Shark Tank investors certainly throw a lot of questions at the entrepreneurs, and one is about their valuation of the company. So, I'm back watching YouTube on my laptop, asking for more information. The following are by Money Week (139). "How to value a company using discounted cash flow" and another "Why do profitable firms go bust?" (140). This one points out that one of the main problems is 'overtrading' which I've always known could be a problem. The presenter is now mentioning 'credit terms' the length of time that buyers demand before they must pay their invoices. Next I'm watching "Ten signs a company's in trouble" (141) and now "The accounting trick that fooled Poly Peck investors" (142). Finally I'm watching "What is a balance sheet?" (143).

Saturday 20th October

I think it might be helpful if I could find a book about social media.

Wednesday 24th October

I've been reading the Writers and Artists Yearbook to try and understand how I can publish my diary on Amazon's Kindle

I'm going to check how to listen to a Radio 4 podcast now which is free to download. So, I've 'searched' 'Money Box Radio 4' and clicked on the episode entitled 'Late Payments'. *Podcast (144).* To listen, type Money Box Late Payments into the Search box and download the episode. This is worth a listen because apparently more than 50,000 small firms go bust each year due to late payments.

VAT is charged at 20% on eBooks but not on hard print copies. For example, on a recent eBook that I purchased for £0.99 the invoice was made up as follows: Unit price net VAT £0.82; VAT rate 20%; unit price including VAT £0.99; total price inclusive of VAT £0.99. VAT rate 20%, VAT amount £0.17.

There's so much of interest to read about publishing, that I really must stop now as it's becoming a distraction. This is a link to the British

Library Business and IP Centre (145) where you can discover their many services. I would recommend reading this page even if you live outside London as their services are spread nationwide it seems with lots of business support. Unfortunately, the link to ISBN codes is currently offline due to some disruption to their website, but you could keep a look out for it or ask the Business Centre staff. However, Amazon does say that they can provide an ISBN for free but I'm not sure yet whether there are any conditions attached. (I've now read that they aren't required for eBooks).

Thursday 25th October

I ordered a book on Social Media Marketing the other day and it's now arrived. I think it's going to take me months to become proficient, so I'd better start reading.

I'm sure I must have typed this before. However, because I had quite a lot of trouble working out why the laptop wouldn't talk to my new printer, I'm going to remind myself again that I needed to download the drivers from the manufacturer's website.

I later had a similar problem after switching Broadband supplier and receiving a new router. I checked via troubleshooting and discovered that there was a driver problem again. So, I spoke to the support centre operative who could only suggest that I check the printer manual. I looked for this online once more. In a nutshell, as the printer was already set up for a wireless connection, I just needed to find the term WLAN on the small printer screen, follow a few on-screen instructions, then press and hold the WLAN button on the router for five seconds, then OK on the printer. WLAN stands for wireless local area network see Wikipedia. (*146).

NOVEMBER

Monday 5th November

Today I'm going to get the X account up and running.

OK, so I'm on Wikipedia and see that tweets are restricted to 280 characters. I need to be registered to post tweets, otherwise I can only read them. I am registered, so that's OK, but I think I'm supposed to activate the account. I can tweet from my computer via the **X** website, via short messaging services (SMS) or smartphone.

OK, so I've just signed in. The first thing I see is a notice about 'Privacy Policy'. (1) Tweets are viewable anywhere in the world. (2) There are also non-public ways to tweet. (3) You can use a pseudonym. (4) The tweeter's IP address is collected. (5) I can share my email address, phone number etc. if I want to. (6) I can use 'settings' to control the data I share with **X,** (need to read more on this). (7) I can download the information I've shared on **X**. (8) **X** will use information gained from my tweets, retweets, read content etc. to send me more relevant content, (I presume this means advertisements), which I can change at any time. And that's about it.

I can ask for more information if I want to, however it doesn't appear to mention photographs or sharing data with third parties which is revealed on Wikipedia, but perhaps I'm not looking hard enough. I've now clicked on 'Terms of Service' and see that there's mention of greater transparency about sharing user information with business partners, also that I can 'deactivate' my **X** account. I'm going to 'Rules and Policies' now. There seems to be a 'search' facility to find content and there's a difference between signing in on the web and on Android apps.

X also wants my mobile phone number, but I'll probably use my laptop. Reading more, this is, they say, so they can send me a code, and then I must use both my password and the code to log-in. It seems I need a profile photograph. I've already put one of these up when registering. My username for logging in seems to have been decided for me and I presume my display name is the same as my gadget brand name.

I'll need to double check all this once I'm ready. It looks as though log-in verification may be optional. It seems that my phone number and email can be 'discoverable' unless I adjust my 'settings'. I'm very glad that I'm reading all this information before I start.

OK, I think I've sorted out the account but haven't activated verification yet as I need to read a bit more.

Tuesday 6th November

I've just sketched an appropriate picture for the front of my Kindle book and sent it to an online artist for a quote.

During my edit, I've come across something that requires further follow-up, so I've just been looking for 'Growth Hubs' (147). (LEP stands for Local Enterprise Partnership). There are more than 38 spread across the UK. (You need to scroll down and click on 'View all – LEP Growth Hubs' to bring up the list.

Friday 9th November

My online artist chum has responded to my request for a front page for my Kindle diary and the price he has quoted is £200 for black and white, £250 for colour with no limit on the number of alterations required.

Monday 19th November

I've just been looking around the Amazon website during today's editing session and have found Amazon 'Print-on-Demand'. It seems that my diary could be printed at a cost of £0.01 per black and white page, £0.45 for the cover in colour and £0.70 for the binding. That makes a total of £3.15 if it's 200 pages long and I presume they're talking about reducing an A4 page down to A5 but I've no idea of spacing etc. or delivery fees at present.

Thursday 22nd November

I've just seen a note on the calendar that the Confirmation Statement is due at Companies House. So, I've gone to their website and am clicking on 'File your Confirmation Statement' (annual return). Clicked on 'Start Now' and signed in with the company email address and the password. The next page says, 'Sign in to a Company'. So, I've typed in the Company Number and beneath it the Authentication Code that I was sent originally. On the next page I can see that the company accounts are up to date and not due until 31st August and that the Confirmation Statement date is today, but must be filed by the 6th of December, latest. There's also mention of the 'payment period'. I've now clicked on 'File Confirmation Statement then START. I'm clicking on the 'view' buttons to see what information I've filed to date. Now I want to find out if there's a more relevant SIC code (*148) for my product, so I've gone back to the Companies House website to look through the categories. I can't find anything more appropriate although it's not quite accurate, so will leave it as that. Everything else remains the same so I've clicked on the 'Submit' button at the bottom.

Now I'm on a page where I'm asked to make a payment of £13, so I've clicked on the 'dot' against 'credit/debit card or PayPal'. I only have a debit card for the company so that I can keep day-to-day control of the finances, although the advice seems to be to only use a credit card for security reasons. Next page – I've just made a note of the 'submission number' and clicked on 'Continue'. I've now clicked on 'Visa card payment' and am on the next page where I'm filling out the details. I've clicked on PAY and the next page says, 'Confirmation and Submission of payment'. So, I'm going to print a copy and file it. The final message at the bottom says that I shall receive confirmation by email.

Wednesday 28th November

I've just received a reminder from HMRC that my Company Tax Return's due imminently so I'm having to jump around a bit.

On checking my most recent bank statements I've found two Amazon credits (I've bought something supposedly) for £25.76 and £14.50 yet when I look at my 'orders placed' page on their website, nothing ties up with these amounts. So, the advice they give is to phone them. As it's a 0800 number I think it must be free, so I'll do that when I get a spare moment.

This is so time consuming. I couldn't believe that I hadn't completed the tax return for the last period, so, I entered the HMRC website again to see if I could find the return that my records told me I'd submitted on the 19th of September. Fortunately, I had a hard copy but couldn't find one online. I also had an email saying that it had been received but it left the question as to whether it had been accepted hanging in the air and said I should check its progress. So, I clicked on 'Accounting Period' just now and used the drop-down menu to see whether I owed them anything. I don't. I think this is all a bit of a mix-up at their end what with everything being done online now. The threat of a £100 fine really made me move!

DECEMBER

Wednesday 5th December

This morning, I decided to see what help The Kings Trust was providing for 18 – 30-year-olds. The first thing I notice is that the website seems to be encouraging self-employment, which is the unregistered company structure mentioned at the beginning. For some reason I'm unable to embed the link to their resources here but they are easy to find if you type 'business tools' into the search box on The Kings Trust home page (149) There's help with business plans and an abundance of other useful advice suitable for those of all ages.

Loans appear to be the primary source of financial help, rather than grants and The Kings Trust is a delivery partner of the Start-up Loans Company. Of course, this could change in time if the government decides it can afford more funding, and I note that there may be a grant available for those who qualify. Taking advantage of all the free resources this organization has to offer, would seem to be an excellent idea for those who want to learn more and self-educate.

Sunday 9th December

Today I can see that there have been visits to the website by YandexBot/3.0, Googlebot/2.1, Googlebot Mobile, bingbot/2.0, BLEXbot/1.0 and AshrefsBot/5.2 which also represents 35% of the total percentage of crawlers who made a visit this week. The following link shows which robots belong to which category and lists 'Search Engine Bots', 'Commercial Crawlers', 'Feed Fetchers' and 'Monitoring bots'; for example, AshrefsBot/5.2 (150) is a 'commercial crawler' gathering marketing information. (Scroll to the bottom and click on 'see full report' for the whole list – all 173 of them!)

I'm continuing my research into ISBNs (International Standard Book Numbers). Firstly, I've discovered that within the first month of publication, a digital copy of my book should be deposited with the British Library but when I called, they said it wasn't necessary for just a single book, but it's best to check if you're planning on becoming a published author. You can find out about ISBNs on their website here (151)

It seems that Amazon will automatically assign an ASIN (Amazon Standard Identification Number) to identify my eBook, but I'll need to get an ISBN if I wish to publish a paperback or hardback other than on Amazon (or that may be as well as; so, do please check)! The ASIN is free, but an ISBN is not. Here are the conditions attached to Amazon's free ISBNs/ASINs (152).

You can buy an ISBN number from Nielson isbn store (154). Nielsen Book runs the ISBN Agency for the UK and Ireland. From what I've read it seems that a single number will cost me £93.00 plus VAT.

To start publishing on Amazon you can click on Amazon Direct Publishing (153).

I'm going to publish the diary on Kindle as soon as it's ready. With regard to VAT which you can read about here GOV.UK (156), it seems this will be deducted by Amazon; (however you really must check this information for yourself.)

I'm going to visit Amazon now. I'm not sure yet whether I'm going to permit the book to be put on Kindle Unlimited (their subscription service where books are free bar the subscription price). From what I've read in my paperback copy of the Writers & Artists Yearbook, publishers/authors are paid per page that's read from a 'pot of money;' but I'm not too clear about all this now.

I've just been reading some advice about how independent book publishers (i.e. people like me) can get their books into our UK libraries, but I've now lost the link. I must remember to follow this up. I think I saw something on Amazon as well. It's probably important to buy an ISBN if I want to go down this route and not use an ASIN.

Moving away from Kindle now, I'm trying to sign in to my 'seller account' on Amazon which is different, and it seems I must go to Seller Central and then sign in using my email or mobile phone number followed by my password. More below:

Thursday 27th December

Today I seem to have much more energy and am better able to focus on the next steps. An email has just arrived from HMRC reminding me that my VAT return is due at the end of December.

I really want to get my gadget onto Amazon. When I was last in Seller Central, they had to verify the business account, so now that they've had time to do this, I'll go back and try to make some progress

First, I'm signing in with the company email address, not the company name. After putting in the password the phone has rung and I've been told my verification number, which I've carefully written down. Anyway, Amazon won't let me sign in, saying that the number/account 'is not recognised'. So, I've clicked on 'didn't receive the number' or something and have been given the option to have the verification number sent to my landline or mobile, or by text; I've chosen text. I'm now in.

Note: FBA stands for fulfilment by Amazon.

This seems worth reading, apparently, I can create a store on Amazon for free. I can drive shoppers to my store with Ads on Amazon. I've now gone into 'Seller University' and will need to spend some time here so will take a break.

Something which has attracted my attention now is that I will have little control over shipping fees, so for this reason I shall need to reduce the selling price to take this into account even though it will make the overall cost seem somewhat unbalanced.

Oh, I thought I'd be able to use PayPal on here like eBay, but it seems not. Now I understand why Amazon needs to verify the company bank account.

Later today… I'm being asked to send a copy of a recent bank statement. I found help with this on the Seller Central forum but I'm reluctant to pass on information here as it involves bank details. It's not difficult – just be cautious. It's the account number and address etc. that they need to verify

I've been editing my diary in Microsoft Word. It seems that I can upload the book to the KDP website via **Bookshelf.**

JANUARY

Tuesday 1st January

Happy New Year!

I think it's now time to consider how much more time, effort and money I should spend on this project and reflect on what I've learned so far.

One thing that I've discovered is that my current lack of control over cost and availability are the most difficult elements to overcome. For this reason, I've no wish to target the high street retail sector for the time being or pursue a wholesale business model.

The UK vending machine sector would appear to be about buying and selling inexpensive last-minute items that customers are familiar with, but nothing more exciting that could be slightly risky for them. Just like regular retailers, they'll need to take something out of the machine, to put an untried product in. So again, this is about proving demand for my item which so far hasn't been possible. There also appears to be a lack of competition in the vending sector and the current system of being paid for goods after they've been sold doesn't work for me. So, this goes on the backburner for now.

Investing in stock to sell on a shopping channel is also too risky even if it would provide some early sales and publicity. In my experience, goods are usually purchased on a sale-or-return basis which would require the company to remove any unsold stock from the channel's warehouse if the full consignment failed to sell. Any over payment would need to be refunded, and the company could be left holding a lot of stock.

Regarding suppliers, it sometimes takes more than one mistake to learn a lesson. I recall that I was once given a price of £300 over the phone for an item which suddenly shot up to £800 once I was committed. On another occasion I received a verbal quote of £30 which was increased to £80 once the job was done. So, in any future dealings with potential suppliers, it's obviously wise to ask for the quote in writing, including the amount of notice they'll be willing to give should they intend to raise their prices.

I'm now mindful that suppliers may initially be pricing low to gain business. If the above precautions are taken, advance notice will provide time to make other arrangements, subject to there being an alternative supplier out there, which there needs to be before I place an order. Anyone can put up a smoke screen and blame the increase on a sudden rise in production costs. This shouldn't be a problem that start-ups have to face so early on!

So, what's left? Well, there's always the option of selling online but the reward needs to be sufficient to make the effort and potential advertising cost worthwhile. So, I'm going to gather all my earlier notes on this topic and thoroughly update my Business Plan to see whether this is a viable option. According to my calculations, my minimum fixed costs per annum selling on Amazon/eBay and my own website, will be in the region of £800 which will include the GTIN (£119 pa ex VAT) keeping the patent in force, website costs and the continued use of the registered office. But I still need to consider insurance as this is a new gadget that I'm producing myself.

As I said earlier, the market seems to be telling me that the public don't yet understand the benefits of my gadget.

The model that I've adopted for this business venture, is unusual, being built around a newly patented product. As you will have seen it's quite complicated, so probably isn't one that the majority would choose to attempt as a first enterprise. Nevertheless, I hope I've managed to demonstrate that learning the ropes is both an interesting and enjoyable challenge. Identifying a key skill that you possess, or a product or service that you can sell, is obviously the key to getting a job, or owning and running your own successful business.

So, I shall end here and wish you well. I hope you have enjoyed this look at the world of work and can see how firms of all shapes and sizes trade with one another

Oops! There's never a dull moment with HMRC – I've just been fined £100!

Printed in Dunstable, United Kingdom

63294001R00131